AI For All

How Everyday People Can Benefit from Artificial Intelligence

Shawn Schuster

Umlaut Publishing

Print ISBN: 978-1-961432-00-0

Ebook ISBN: 978-1-961432-01-7

BISAC:

BUS012000   **BUSINESS & ECONOMICS** / Careers / General

COM042000   **COMPUTERS** / Artificial Intelligence / Natural Language Processing

SEL021000   **SELF-HELP** / Motivational & Inspirational

Contents

Chapter One

Introduction to Artificial Intelligence

Artificial Intelligence is taking our jobs and invading our privacy! At least that's what some folks would like you to think. The fact is, we're at such a crucial time in AI's rapid development that we face some uncertain times in just about every sector. AI may not always take the form we see today, but there's no denying that it will shape our lives for the next few generations until it becomes so commonplace, we don't even think about its integration into modern society.

Right now, I think it's safe to say that we're currently in the Wild West of this technology. Imagine, if you will, that it's 1849 and you've heard talk that gold has been discovered out past the Rockies in California. We can all get a piece of our own private fortune if we load up our wagons and head out toward the setting sun. But hurry! Hundreds of thousands of other people are doing the same thing, and not everyone will find what they're looking for.

The problem is, no one knows about the path leading from here to there. No one knows the dangers and obstacles that make the journey difficult without a proper guide.

And that's why I wrote this book. I'm not a Natural Language Processing (NLP) scholar nor do I have a degree in robotics, but I am a business owner who realizes the potential that this booming technology can have on our economy. I firmly believe, as we sit here trying to figure out how this brand new economic landscape can recover from a global pandemic that sent everyone into work-from-home mode, AI is the one thing we need to dig us out of the quicksand, dust off our hats, and lead us through to a proverbial Sutter's Mill. There's gold in them thar hills!

The year of this book's publication (2023) has already seen incredible growth in not only the applications of AI, but also the general public's awareness of what it can do. Despite the fact that AI has been around since the 1950s, we're just now seeing its true potential. And it's indescribably promising.

Now, before you read any further, let me address the elephant in the room. As I sit here, telling you how beneficial AI is to workflows, marketing, and idea planning, you might wonder if this entire book was just one big text output from ChatGPT. After all, if I'm using this book to explain how beneficial AI can be for your projects, wouldn't it make sense to use that same tool to create this entire project? Just type in a few instructions and BAM! The finished product comes right out fully formatted and ready to print, right?

Not exactly. Chances are, this scenario will eventually be possible (probably sooner than later), but I will readily admit that AI is not entirely to that point just yet. That said, AI did help me form an outline, generate a few key ideas, and guide me through some creative word choices along the way. It would be silly for me not to practice what I preach, but I feel like that's the point. As you read this book, realize that the techniques I used to get this book into your hands are the same techniques that you can use to improve your own business. That's not to say that AI should do it for you, but it should help make the process better.

If that idea scares you, I hope this book can convince you that AI should be considered just another tool of the creative process. But if the idea excites you, then you may already be aware of its benefits, and I'm sure you're excited by the possibilities.

Either way, you're in for a real treat!

How to Use This Book

While you're certainly welcome to read this book cover to cover, I wrote it with the intention of allowing people to skip around and read about how AI can benefit their specific industry. Whether you're starting a small business or are part of a larger corporation, I firmly believe that AI can help anyone looking to streamline their process.

Each chapter of this book from Chapter 3 to Chapter 15 is broken down by industry to make it easier to pick and choose which topics apply to you most accurately. I also cover important topics such as ethical concerns, limitations of the technology, and where we should go from here.

What is AI?

Artificial intelligence (AI) is a branch of computer science that deals with creating intelligent machines that can perform tasks that usually require human intelligence, such as learning, problem-solving, and decision-making. In other words, AI enables machines to perform cognitive functions that are typically associated with human beings.

At its core, AI works by using algorithms and statistical models to analyze data and make predictions or decisions. It can be broken down into several categories, including machine learning, natural language processing, computer vision, and robotics.

Machine learning is a type of AI that allows machines to learn from experience and improve their performance over time. This is done by feeding large amounts of data into algorithms, which then adjust their parameters to improve their accuracy in predicting outcomes. Machine learning is used in a wide range of applications, such as image recognition, speech recognition, and recommendation systems.

Natural language processing (NLP) is another type of AI that enables machines to understand and interpret human language. NLP algorithms can be used to analyze and extract meaning from text, speech, and other forms of communication. This technology is used in applications such as virtual assistants, chatbots, and language translation software.

Computer vision is an area of AI that focuses on enabling machines to interpret and analyze visual information. This can include tasks such as image recognition, object detection, and facial recognition. Computer vision is used in a variety of applications, such as self-driving cars, security systems, and medical imaging.

Finally, robotics is a type of AI that involves creating physical machines that can perform tasks autonomously. Robots can be programmed to perform tasks such as assembly line work, cleaning, and even surgery.

In the modern world, AI has a wide range of capabilities that are already being used in numerous applications. For example, machine learning algorithms are used to personalize recommendations on websites like Amazon and Netflix, while NLP is used in virtual assistants like Siri and Alexa. Computer vision is used in security systems and self-driving cars, and robotics is used in manufacturing and healthcare.

Overall, AI has the potential to revolutionize the way we live and work, but it also presents ethical and societal challenges that need to be carefully considered and addressed. We'll get to that in a bit, but first, let's explore how it all got started.

The History of AI

The history of AI dates back to the mid-20th century when researchers began to explore the possibility of creating machines that could perform tasks that required human intelligence. The origins of AI can be traced back to the Dartmouth Conference in 1956, where the term "artificial intelligence" was coined.

Early research in AI was heavily influenced by the work of mathematician Alan Turing, who proposed the concept of a machine that could perform any intellectual task that a human could. In the years that followed, a number of pioneering researchers made significant contributions to the development of AI.

One of the most significant early figures in AI was John McCarthy, who is often referred to as the "father of AI". McCarthy was a computer scientist who helped organize the Dartmouth Conference and was instrumental in developing the first programming language specifically for AI, called LISP.

Another important figure in the early days of AI was Marvin Minsky, who was a co-founder of the AI laboratory at MIT. Minsky was interested in developing machines that could learn from experience and was one of the pioneers of the subfield of AI known as machine learning.

Other notable researchers in the early days of AI include Claude Shannon, who is known for his work on information theory, and Herbert Simon, who was interested in the problem of decision-making.

In the 1960s and 1970s, AI research began to make significant strides, with the development of expert systems and other forms of AI technology. However, progress in the field slowed in the 1980s and 1990s, as researchers encountered significant challenges in developing machines that could reason and understand language.

In the realm of AI-generated art, one notable researcher was Harold Cohen who created a computer program called AARON in 1972. The program is thought to be the first ever to create autonomous art from a machine, as showcased in Cohen's 1983 book, "The First Artificial Intelligence Coloring Book."

Cohen's work was certainly ahead of its time as the artist himself ceased development on the project when he concluded that the C programming language wasn't capable of dealing with the complex concept of color well enough. One can't help but wonder what Cohen would think of something like Midjourney today!

In recent years, advances in machine learning and other forms of AI have led to significant breakthroughs in areas such as image and speech recognition, natural language processing, and robotics. Today, AI is a rapidly growing field with applications in a wide range of industries, including healthcare, finance, and transportation.

Later in this book, we'll explore more specific applications for AI as it pertains to certain job fields.

Chapter Two

Understanding AI: Is it Friend or Foe?

While many might believe that AI is out to take over the world and cause the next apocalyptic event, the truth is that it was developed to make our lives easier and more efficient.

AI technology is designed and programmed by humans to perform specific tasks, and it can only do what it has been programmed to do. Therefore, humans are ultimately responsible for the actions of AI and can control its use. For now.

It's also important to note that AI is a neutral technology, and is not inherently good or evil. It is simply a tool that can be used for either positive or negative purposes. The way we use AI is up to us, and we can design it to benefit society and improve our lives.

But with that said, there are certainly instances of bias that have been found in the AI's programming. This bias is the result of human beings and not something created in an artificial imagination. Can we ever get to the point where AI can be so sentient that it creates its own theories and beliefs? I'm sure we will, but we're just not to that point yet.

Geoffrey Hinton, who is often called the grandfather of AI, thanks to his pioneering work on artificial neural networks in the 1980s and later at Google, recently stated that he was afraid of the potential dangers of AI in the wrong hands. His retirement from Google in May of 2023 was sparked by his concern that the AI tech race between Microsoft and Google might become a problem very soon if left unchecked.

While Hinton's concerns are certainly valid considering the fact that he probably knows more about the technology than most of the world, I feel like regulations are coming soon. Do I welcome regulations? Not entirely, but I feel like it's inevitable as the largest players in the tech space are already calling for a "slow-down" of AI's growth.

But how is that possible? If the tech giants slow down their AI development, won't someone else come along and pick up where they left off? And what will their intentions be? AI development can't exactly be stopped at this point, which is both exciting and intimidating.

What are the different types of AI?

There are generally three types of AI: narrow or weak AI, general or strong AI, and artificial superintelligence.

Narrow or Weak AI

Narrow or weak AI refers to artificial intelligence systems that are designed to perform specific tasks or solve particular problems. These systems are "narrow" or "weak" because they are limited in their abilities and can only perform the specific task they were programmed to do.

For example, a speech recognition system that can accurately transcribe spoken words is a narrow AI system because it can only perform that one specific task. Similarly, a chess-playing program that can beat human players is a narrow AI system because it is designed to excel at that one specific task.

These systems can be very powerful and useful in specific domains, but they are not capable of learning or adapting to new tasks or situations beyond what they were designed for. Examples of narrow AI include virtual assistants like Siri and Alexa, self-driving cars, and recommendation algorithms used by online shopping websites.

While all of these examples were certainly impressive years ago, they're now already considered the most basic functions of AI.

General or Strong AI

General or strong AI is where we are on the AI timeline today. It refers to artificial intelligence systems that are designed to perform any intellectual task that a human can. These systems are "strong" or "general" because they are capable of understanding and learning any cognitive task that a human can, and can apply that understanding to a wide range of different tasks and situations.

For example, a strong or general AI system could learn to recognize speech, understand natural language, read and interpret images and videos, and perform any other cognitive task that a human can. Moreover, it would be able to learn and adapt to new tasks and situations on its own, without the need for human intervention or programming.

The goal of strong or general AI is to create machines that can think and reason like humans, with the ability to understand and interact with the world in a way that is indistinguishable from human intelligence. While there have been significant advances in AI research in recent years, achieving "true" strong or general AI remains a significant challenge and is still the subject of ongoing research and development.

Artificial Superintelligence

Artificial superintelligence (ASI) refers to AI that is more advanced than human intelligence. It is capable of self-improvement and can surpass human reasoning and cognitive abilities. While ASI is still purely hypothetical, many researchers believe that it could have significant implications for the future of humanity.

Artificial superintelligence is often associated with the concept of a "singularity," which refers to a hypothetical point in the future when artificial intelligence will surpass human intelligence and lead to a rapid and unprecedented acceleration in technological progress.

Some examples of ASI would potentially include:

1. Solving complex problems: ASI could be used to solve incredibly complex problems in science, engineering, and other fields. For example, ASI might be able to develop new theories in physics or chemistry that humans haven't yet been able to discover.

2. Designing advanced technology: ASI could be used to design advanced technologies that we can't even imagine today. For example, ASI might be able to develop nanobots that could repair damaged cells in the human body or create entirely new materials with unique properties.

3. Understanding and predicting human behavior: ASI could be used to understand and predict human behavior in ways that are currently impossible. For example, ASI might be able to analyze massive amounts of data to predict political trends or social movements.

4. Developing self-improving AI: ASI could be capable of creating even more advanced AI systems, leading

to an exponential increase in intelligence. This could eventually result in an intelligence explosion, where AI becomes so advanced that it is beyond human comprehension.

The idea of artificial superintelligence raises significant questions about the future of humanity and the role that intelligent machines may play in shaping our society. While many experts believe that the development of artificial superintelligence is still a long way off, there is no doubt that it represents a major challenge and opportunity for the field of artificial intelligence and for humanity as a whole.

What Are Some Advantages of AI?

Alright, so now you understand what AI is, but you want to understand what it can do for you specifically. This concept is the main reason I wrote this book as I believe that many people misunderstand how AI could be a beneficial technology – especially in business.

Artificial Intelligence has a number of advantages in both the present and the future, but we're just now realizing a few of the more important ones as the technology improves.

Increased Efficiency

One of the primary benefits of AI is that it can help automate routine tasks and processes, increasing efficiency and reducing the need for human intervention. This can save time and money and allow individuals and organizations to focus on higher-level tasks that require more complex reasoning and decision-making.

The automation industry could certainly stand to benefit from AI systems that can automate repetitive and time-consuming tasks that would otherwise be done manually by humans. For example, in manufacturing, AI-powered robots can assemble products at a much faster rate than humans, reducing production time and costs.

In data analysis applications, AI can analyze vast amounts of data in real-time, identifying patterns and insights that humans might miss. This can help businesses make data-driven decisions, optimize processes, and improve customer experience.

A perfect example of this is AI-powered chatbots that can provide 24/7 customer support, answering common questions and resolving issues in real-time. This can reduce wait times for customers and free up human support agents to focus on more complex issues.

There are also several job-specific benefits to the technology which I'll cover in more depth later in this book.

Improved Accuracy

AI algorithms can analyze large amounts of data and make accurate predictions or recommendations based on that data. This can be particularly useful in fields such as healthcare, where AI can help doctors diagnose diseases and plan treatments by analyzing patient data such as medical history, lab results, and imaging scans. This can lead to more accurate diagnoses, better treatment plans, and improved patient outcomes.

Fraud detection is another big one for accuracy. AI-powered systems can analyze large amounts of data to identify patterns and anomalies that indicate fraudulent activity. This can help prevent financial losses and improve security for individuals and businesses.

In quality control situations, AI can monitor production processes in real-time, identifying defects and issues that might not be visible to human operators. This can lead to higher-quality products and fewer recalls.

Weather forecasting accuracy is certainly a welcome benefit of AI as the tech can process large amounts of weather data from sensors and satellites to generate accurate weather forecasts more quickly than ever before. This can help individuals and businesses plan for severe weather events and make informed decisions based on weather conditions.

While AI has already helped with language translation for many years, modern AI-powered systems can translate text and speech between different languages more accurately than ever – even through audio and by mimicking regional accents. This can help to break down language barriers and facilitate better communication between people from different backgrounds.

Personalization

AI can be used to create custom experiences for individuals, such as personalized product recommendations, tailored marketing messages, and individual healthcare plans that cater to each patient. This can help individuals get the products and services that meet their specific needs and preferences.

By analyzing a person's purchase history, browsing behavior, and other data, AI can recommend products or services that are likely to appeal to them. This can create a more personalized shopping experience and increase the likelihood of repeat business.

AI can also analyze a person's viewing or listening history to recommend content that is likely to interest them. This can be used in a variety of contexts, from music streaming services to video platforms like YouTube or Netflix.

That information can also be used to serve consumers targeted ads that are more likely to resonate with them. This can create a more relevant and engaging advertising experience, while also increasing the effectiveness of advertising campaigns.

A person's medical history and genetic data can also be used to create personalized treatment plans that are tailored to their specific needs. This can improve treatment outcomes and reduce the likelihood of adverse reactions to medications.

Better Decision-Making

AI can aid humans in the decision-making process by analyzing large amounts of data, identifying patterns and trends, and providing insights and recommendations that can help humans make more informed decisions. Here are some examples:

1. Data analysis: AI algorithms can be used to analyze large datasets from multiple sources, identifying patterns and trends that humans may not be able to detect on their own. This information can be used to inform decision-making in a wide range of fields, from finance to healthcare to marketing.

2. Risk assessment: AI can be used to assess risk in a variety of contexts, from financial investments to public safety. By analyzing data and identifying potential risks, AI can help humans make better decisions and reduce the likelihood of negative outcomes.

3. Prediction: AI can be used to predict future outcomes based on historical data and current trends. This information can be used to inform decision-making in a variety of contexts, from sports betting to weather forecasting to investments.

Improved Safety

AI can be used to improve safety in a variety of contexts, such as self-driving cars that can help reduce the number of accidents on the road, or robots that can perform dangerous tasks in environments typically hazardous to humans. But the possibilities branch out quite significantly from there.

If you've ever worked in an industrial facility and dealt with heavy equipment or machinery, you understand the importance of preventative maintenance. Heck, even the machine we use to get to work every day (our car) needs regular check-ups.

AI algorithms can be used to predict when equipment or infrastructure is likely to fail, allowing maintenance crews (or your local mechanic) to address potential safety issues before they become a problem. This can help prevent accidents and ensure that critical systems are always working properly.

By analyzing real-time data from sensors and other sources, AI algorithms can predict when equipment is likely to fail, allowing for preventative maintenance to be scheduled in advance. This can help avoid unexpected downtime and reduce repair costs.

When equipment does fail, AI can be used to diagnose the root cause of the problem. By analyzing data from sensors and historical maintenance records, AI algorithms can identify the most likely cause of the failure and provide guidance to maintenance teams on how to fix the issue.

AI can also help emergency responders quickly assess the extent of damage caused by natural disasters, such as earthquakes or hurricanes. This can help them determine where to send resources and how to allocate them most effectively, potentially saving lives in the process.

While the idea of AI-powered cameras might scare most people, they can be used to monitor public spaces and detect potential safety threats, such as unattended packages or suspicious behavior. This can help security personnel respond quickly to potential threats and prevent them from escalating into more serious incidents.

In the context of traffic safety, AI algorithms can be used to analyze traffic patterns and identify areas where accidents are more likely to occur. This information can be used to improve road design, install safety features, and target public awareness campaigns to improve driver behavior and reduce accidents.

What are the Limitations of AI?

As I admittedly spend a good chunk of this book focusing on the positive aspects of AI, we also have to consider the fact that there are certain limitations.

Lack of Common Sense

AI systems are designed to perform tasks by following a set of predefined rules and algorithms. They can be trained to recognize patterns, make predictions, and even learn from new data. However, AI systems often lack common sense, which is a human-like ability to understand and apply practical knowledge in everyday situations.

Common sense helps us humans make heads or tails of the world around us, and to use our knowledge and experiences to make informed decisions. It allows us to understand that water is wet, fire is hot, and that we should not stick our hands in moving lawnmower blades. These are things that most people take for granted, but they are not necessarily intuitive for machines.

Without common sense, AI systems can make mistakes or produce unexpected results when faced with new or unusual situations. For example, a self-driving car that is programmed to avoid collisions might still crash into a tree if it encounters a situation that is not covered by its rules. Similarly, a language translation system might produce a nonsensical output if it encounters a phrase or idiom that it has not been trained to understand.

In addition, lack of common sense also limits the ability of AI systems to interact with humans in a natural and intuitive way. Humans often rely on context, social cues, and implicit knowledge to communicate effectively, but these are difficult to model in AI systems.

Therefore, developing AI systems with common sense is an important research area in AI. Advancements in natural language processing, computer vision, and other fields are helping to address this limitation, but it remains a challenging problem that will require significant research and development efforts.

Lack of a Sense of Humor

While the same could be said for many humans, AI lacks a true sense of humor. Sure, it can recite and understand jokes and riddles to a degree, but the deeper nuances of humor are often lost on AI.

Humor is a complex human trait that involves understanding and interpreting social and cultural contexts, nuances of language, and emotional cues. These are all areas where AI is still developing and improving. I suggest feeding the first seven seasons of The Office (American) into the greater algorithm, but that's just me.

Additionally, humor is subjective and can vary greatly depending on individual preferences and cultural differences. What one person finds funny, another may not. This can make it challenging for AI to accurately and consistently recognize and produce humor that will be universally understood and appreciated.

While AI may not yet have a sense of humor in the same way that humans do, there are efforts underway to develop AI-powered tools that can generate humorous content, such as chatbots or virtual assistants that can tell jokes or respond with witty remarks. However, these tools are still in the early stages of development and are not yet capable of replicating the full range of human humor.

Limited Creativity

While AI can be used to create art, music, and other imaginative works, it still lacks the creativity and intuition of human artists. AI-generated works may lack the emotional depth and nuance of human-created art.

Human creativity allows us to come up with original and innovative ideas, which are not just a combination of existing concepts, as is the case with AI. It involves the ability to think outside the box, see things from a different perspective, and make intuitive connections between seemingly unrelated concepts. These abilities are essential for many tasks, such as art, music, design, and even scientific discovery.

While AI can be trained to generate new ideas, it is limited by the data it has been trained on. This means that it can only generate ideas based on the patterns it has learned from the data. If an AI model is trained on a dataset of paintings, it might be able to generate new paintings that resemble the ones in the dataset, but it is unlikely to create something truly original and innovative. This is a very important distinction that is the basis of a majority of the AI hate from the general public.

Moreover, AI is not capable of experiencing emotions, which are often a source of inspiration for creative work. Emotions can drive creativity by providing motivation, inspiration, and a way to express feelings and experiences. Without emotions, AI lacks the depth of experience necessary for true creative expression.

To overcome the limitations of AI in creativity, researchers are exploring different approaches such as combining AI with human creativity, developing AI models that can learn from small datasets, and training AI models to be more imaginative and open-ended. Some researchers are using generative adversarial networks (GANs) to generate novel and creative content, while others are developing AI models that can interact with humans to co-create new ideas. These approaches hold promise for the future of AI, but the challenge of producing truly creative AI remains a significant one.

Data Dependence

AI algorithms rely on large amounts of data to make decisions, which means that they may struggle in situations where data is limited or incomplete. This can be particularly problematic in fields such as medicine, where AI may not have access to all of the relevant patient data.

AI systems can only operate within the scope of the data they have been trained on. This means that they may struggle to deal with novel situations or contexts that are not represented in the training data.

Plus, the process of collecting, cleaning, and labeling large amounts of data can be expensive and time-consuming. We see these types of limitations now with ChatGPT outages and

Midjourney's recent removal of the free trial to allow the limited bandwidth to be focused on paying members of the service. This can be a significant barrier to entry for smaller organizations or those with limited resources.

To address these limitations, researchers are exploring new techniques for training AI systems with smaller amounts of data and processing power. By addressing these challenges, we can help ensure that AI systems are more robust, reliable, and trustworthy.

Lack of Empathy

AI algorithms lack empathy, which means that they may not be able to understand the emotional needs or perspectives of humans. This can be particularly problematic in fields such as customer service, where empathy and emotional intelligence are critical.

Without empathy, AI systems may struggle to understand the needs and emotions of humans. This can lead to misunderstandings and miscommunications, which can have negative consequences for the user.

In healthcare, for example, patients often require emotional support in addition to medical treatment. AI systems may be able to provide medical advice, but they are not capable of providing the same level of emotional support as a human caregiver.

Another unfortunate example would be if an AI-powered chatbot provides an insensitive response to a user who is grieving or going through a difficult time. That's a tough situation, and could ultimately result in even more distrust of the technology.

To address these limitations, researchers are exploring ways to incorporate empathy into AI systems, such as by training them on emotional data or developing systems that can recognize and respond to human emotions. By doing so, we can ensure that AI systems are better equipped to meet the needs of humans in a variety of settings.

But the crucial question remains: whose emotional data and empathic biases will be used to train the AI?

Security and Privacy Concerns

As AI becomes more advanced, there is a risk that it could be used for malicious purposes, such as hacking or surveillance. This raises important ethical and privacy concerns that must be addressed.

AI systems rely on vast amounts of data, including sensitive personal information, such as financial data, medical records, and biometric data. If an AI system is breached, this data could be compromised, leading to identity theft or other forms of fraud.

There's also the issue of profiling humans. AI systems can be used to create detailed profiles of individuals based on their behavior, preferences, and other data points that can be used for targeted advertising, but it could also be used for more nefarious purposes, such as discrimination or surveillance.

Bias and Discrimination

AI algorithms are only as unbiased as the data they are trained on. If the data contains biases or discriminatory patterns, these biases can be amplified by the AI algorithm (see also: lack of empathy). This can result in unfair or discriminatory outcomes in fields such as hiring or lending.

Politics is a hot-button issue that could also be programmed into the system's algorithm, resulting in biased news feeds and a potential rewrite of historical data. Do we really want AI writing our history books? I would hope not.

Overall, while AI has made significant progress in recent years, there are still some limitations to the technology. These limitations highlight the importance of developing AI in a responsible and ethical manner, and of ensuring that humans remain in control of the technology. Do we need an updated and more advanced AI ethics board? I predict that we'll be heading in that direction soon.

Will AI Take Away My Job?

This is a tough one since it's inevitable that any progress will both add and remove jobs. Think back to the industries of 20 years ago and how many of those are now obsolete. From film developers to video rental store clerks, the progression of technology has eliminated several jobs (even entire industries) in recent years, but others have risen up in unexpected ways.

From self check-out stations to self-serve gas pumps to ATMS and beyond, the progression of technology has certainly replaced some jobs, but opened up the door for many more. Someone has to maintain, repair, design, and construct those more advanced stations and entire industries have been built around that type of work.

Much of this book highlights ways to utilize AI to enhance your business and personal lives. With the proper understanding of how AI could impact your chosen industry or career, you're one step ahead of those who resist that progression. And together, by weighing every angle of AI's impact on the future, we can make it work for us instead of against us.

Chapter Three

AI for Business

AI is used in business operations and decision-making to automate and optimize various processes, reduce costs, increase efficiency, and provide valuable insights to make better-informed decisions.

In 2023, knowledge of AI systems like GPT-4 is actually showing up as a requirement on a high percentage of job listings. Employers who are learning the importance of these AI chatbots want to hire people with the skills to turn this technology into profit.

We're going to talk about some of these specific jobs throughout this book, but even as I write this, it's inevitable that new positions are being created specifically for wrangling AI.

Customer Service

AI-powered customer service is a powerful tool that businesses can use to improve their customer experience, reduce costs, and gain insights into customer behavior. One of the main benefits of using AI for customer service is improved response times. AI-powered chatbots can provide instantaneous responses to customer inquiries, 24/7, which means that customers can get help immediately, without needing to wait for a human customer service representative to be available. This can improve customer satisfaction and reduce the likelihood of customers becoming frustrated or dissatisfied with the service they receive.

There are also the cost savings to consider. Hiring additional customer service representatives can be expensive, but chatbots can handle a large volume of routine inquiries and tasks, freeing up human representatives to handle more complex issues. This can reduce costs for businesses and allow them to allocate resources more efficiently.

AI-powered chatbots can also provide a more personalized customer experience. AI algorithms can analyze customer data and personalize responses based on the individual customer's history and preferences. This can help businesses build stronger relationships with their customers and improve customer loyalty. Additionally, AI-powered chatbots can provide customer service support around the clock, even outside of normal business hours. This means that customers can get help when they need it, regardless of the time of day.

Consistency is key, as they say. AI-powered chatbots can provide consistent responses to customer inquiries, ensuring that all customers receive the same level of service. This can help businesses maintain a high standard of customer service across all customer interactions.

Supply Chain Management

The use of AI in supply chain management is becoming increasingly popular as it offers a number of benefits to businesses. One of the key benefits is improved efficiency. AI algorithms can analyze data from a variety of sources, including inventory levels, production rates, and shipping times, and use this data to optimize the supply chain process. This can help businesses reduce lead times, minimize inventory costs, and improve order fulfillment rates.

The increased visibility of AI tools allows businesses to get real-time insights into their supply chain operations. This can help the business identify bottlenecks, track inventory levels, and improve forecasting accuracy. With better visibility, businesses can make more informed decisions about their supply chain operations, which can improve efficiency and reduce costs.

AI can also help businesses identify and mitigate supply chain risks. AI algorithms can analyze data from a variety of sources, including weather forecasts, economic data, and social media trends, to identify potential risks to the supply chain. This can help businesses take proactive measures to mitigate these risks, such as rerouting shipments or increasing inventory levels.

There's also the benefit of improved customer service. Businesses can provide real-time updates on order status and delivery times, which can improve customer satisfaction. Additionally,

AI can help businesses identify trends and patterns in customer behavior, which can help them improve their product offerings and customer service processes.

Of course, all of this can help businesses reduce costs in the long run. By optimizing supply chain processes, businesses can reduce inventory costs, transportation costs, and labor costs. This can result in significant cost savings over time, which can improve the bottom line.

Marketing

AI can offer a range of benefits to businesses when it comes to marketing. One key advantage is improved targeting. AI algorithms can analyze customer data and behavior to create highly targeted and personalized marketing campaigns. By understanding customer preferences and behaviors, businesses can deliver more relevant and personalized marketing messages that are more likely to result in conversions.

AI-powered tools can automate many aspects of the marketing process, including lead generation, content creation, and social media management. This can save businesses time and resources, allowing them to focus on more strategic aspects of their marketing campaigns.

AI can also help businesses analyze and interpret large amounts of data. By using AI-powered analytics tools, businesses can gain valuable insights into customer behavior, marketing campaign effectiveness, and overall marketing ROI (Return on Investment). This can help businesses make more informed decisions about their marketing strategies and improve their overall performance.

Identifying and responding to customer needs in real-time is a big one on this list. AI-powered chatbots and virtual assistants can provide 24/7 customer support and help businesses respond to customer inquiries and concerns quickly and efficiently. This can improve customer satisfaction and help businesses build stronger relationships with their customers.

All of this can help businesses stay ahead of the competition. By using AI-powered tools to analyze industry trends and monitor competitor activity, businesses can identify new opportunities and stay up-to-date with the latest marketing strategies and tactics. This can help them remain competitive in a constantly evolving marketplace.

Fraud Detection

Fraud detection is a critical aspect of any business, and AI can offer significant benefits in this area. AI can detect patterns that may not be apparent to humans. By using machine learning and predictive analytics, AI-powered fraud detection systems can quickly identify potential fraud and take action to prevent it.

AI-powered fraud detection systems can automate many aspects of the fraud detection process, including data analysis, monitoring, and reporting.

AI can also help businesses detect and respond to fraud in real time by quickly identifying suspicious activity and taking action to prevent further damage. This can help businesses minimize losses and protect their reputation.

As businesses grow and expand, they may encounter new and more complex forms of fraud. AI-powered fraud detection systems can scale to meet the needs of larger businesses and can adapt to changing fraud patterns over time.

By using AI-powered fraud detection tools to seek out and prevent fraud, businesses can protect their assets and maintain the trust of their customers. This can help them remain competitive in a marketplace where trust and security are becoming increasingly important.

Nonprofits and Charities

One of the most significant ways in which AI can benefit nonprofits is by improving donor engagement and fundraising. AI can help nonprofits to personalize donor communications, identify potential new donors, and predict donor behavior, leading to more effective fundraising efforts.

Automating administrative tasks, such as data entry and financial reporting, also allows staff to focus on more strategic work in a nonprofit situation. AI can help nonprofits to analyze data and gain insights about their stakeholders, donors, and impact in more efficient ways than ever before.

However, there are unique challenges that nonprofits face with the usage of AI. One challenge is the cost of implementing and maintaining AI technology, which may be a significant investment for nonprofit organizations with limited resources. Additionally, there may be concerns about data privacy and ethical considerations related to the use of AI in decision-making.

Another challenge is ensuring that AI is aligned with the mission and values of the nonprofit organization. Nonprofits must ensure that the use of AI is transparent, fair, and accountable and that it does not perpetuate biases or reinforce existing power imbalances.

AI has the potential to benefit nonprofit entities by making their work more efficient and effective, but nonprofits must carefully consider the unique challenges they face when implementing AI, including cost, data privacy, ethical considerations, and alignment with their mission and values. By carefully considering these challenges and implementing AI in a responsible and transparent way, nonprofits can leverage the power of AI to improve their impact and achieve their mission.

Chapter Four

AI as a Personal Assistant

Having an AI personal assistant may seem like something straight out of a futuristic sci-fi movie, but the reality is that the technology is already here. Aside from simple recommendation and internet search algorithms, AI is capable of so much more that could help you and your business.

How Can AI Be Your Next Personal Assistant?

AI has the potential to be the perfect personal assistant for a busy executive, as it can automate many of the tasks that would typically require the attention of a human assistant.

Scheduling

AI can also help businesses optimize their schedules by analyzing all types of time-sensitive data such as employee availability, customer demand, and business priorities. The schedules developed by AI can maximize productivity and profitability.

AI-powered scheduling tools are especially efficient at adapting to changing business conditions and quickly adjusting schedules based on real-time data. This can help businesses respond to unexpected events and minimize disruptions to their operations.

AI can also help businesses improve employee satisfaction. By using AI-powered scheduling tools that take into account employee preferences and availability, businesses can develop schedules that are fair and accommodating. This can lead to higher levels of employee engagement, retention, and productivity.

By optimizing schedules, businesses can reduce over-staffing and under-staffing, which can lead to cost savings over time.

Email Management

AI can provide several benefits to businesses when it comes to email management. With AI-powered email management tools, businesses can automate various email-related tasks, such as sorting and prioritizing emails, drafting responses, and scheduling follow-ups.

Personally, I'm the type to dread writing email responses beyond "OK, sounds good." I know that my business associates might appreciate a response that sounds a little more heartfelt, so I'll (ironically) turn to AI to turbo-boost what I'm trying to say.

So let's do just that. Let's run "OK, sounds good" through ChatGPT to see how it could possibly improve that award-winning response. These are my favorites:

1. Thank you for the update. I appreciate it.

2. That's great news. Let's proceed as planned.

3. I agree with your proposal. Let's move forward.

4. Sounds like a plan. Thank you for letting me know.

5. I'm on board with this. Thanks for the heads up.

6. Perfect. I'm looking forward to it.

7. Thanks for your prompt response. Let's get started.

How great is that? If you're feeling extra saucy, you can even ask ChatGPT to add in a few emojis for that extra flavor.

In addition to email responses, AI can also help your business improve the security and compliance of your emails by detecting and blocking suspicious or fraudulent emails, such as phishing attempts. This can help businesses protect their data and reputation and comply with regulations.

And who doesn't like studying the stats? By analyzing data such as open rates, click-through rates, and response rates, businesses can develop strategies to improve email engagement and conversion rates over time.

Research

AI can act as a personal assistant and help businesses with research tasks such as gathering information, summarizing data, and identifying patterns.

By using AI-powered research tools that can understand natural language processing (NLP), businesses can gather and analyze data from a wide range of sources, such as online databases, research papers, and news articles. This can help businesses stay up-to-date on industry trends and gain insights into customer behavior.

The AI-powered tools can also analyze customer feedback, allowing businesses to identify patterns and trends in customer behavior and preferences, which ultimately helps businesses develop products and services that meet customer needs and preferences.

Let's not forget about your competition. It's always important to have a leg up on your competitors (especially the ones who don't know about AI), so you can easily utilize AI-powered tools that monitor competitors' online activity and social media presence, allowing your business to gain insights into the competitors' strategies and develop new strategies to stay competitive.

Data Analysis

Artificial Intelligence has revolutionized the way we interact with technology, and it has also transformed the business landscape. One of the most significant benefits of using AI as a personal assistant for data analysis is that it can automate the process. Data analysis involves collecting, organizing, and interpreting large volumes of data.

Traditionally, this process was manual and time-consuming. However, AI can automate many of these tasks, making the process faster, more accurate, and less labor-intensive.

This includes complex analysis tasks that would be difficult or impossible for humans to perform, such as analyzing vast amounts of data to identify patterns, correlations, and anomalies that might go unnoticed by humans. This level of analysis can provide businesses with a more detailed and nuanced understanding of their operations, which can lead to more informed decision-making.

And all of this can be done in real-time! AI algorithms can provide immediate feedback and recommendations to business owners and managers. For example, if there is a sudden drop in sales or a spike in customer complaints, an AI-powered personal assistant can alert the appropriate team members and provide suggestions for how to address the issue.

With recent improvements to AI, you'll find that it can even learn and adapt to the needs of the business over time. As the AI assistant processes more data and interacts with users, it can become more intelligent and better able to provide insights and recommendations that are tailored to the specific needs of the business. This continuous learning and adaptation process can help businesses stay ahead of the competition and make better-informed decisions.

Virtual Assistants

AI-powered virtual assistants, such as Siri and Alexa, already provide hands-free assistance with tasks such as setting reminders, making phone calls, and sending messages. It's inevitable that these "lower" forms of AI will improve over time.

By automating these tasks, AI can free up a businessperson's time to focus on high-level tasks such as strategy and decision-making. Additionally, AI can work around the clock, meaning that tasks can be completed even when the businessperson is not available. This can help increase productivity and efficiency, while also reducing stress and burnout.

Examples of AI Assistant Applications

Here are some examples of AI-based personal assistant apps and their features as of 2023:

Google Assistant: Google Assistant is an AI-based personal assistant app that is available on Android and iOS devices. Its features include:

1. Voice recognition and natural language processing for hands-free assistance

2. Integration with Google services such as Google Calendar, Google Maps, and Google Search

3. Ability to set reminders, make phone calls, send messages, and control smart home devices

4. Personalized recommendations based on user preferences and habits

Siri: Siri is an AI-based personal assistant app that is exclusive to Apple devices. Its features include:

1. Voice recognition and natural language processing for hands-free assistance

2. Integration with Apple services such as Apple Music, Apple Maps, and iMessage

3. Ability to set reminders, make phone calls, send messages, and control smart home devices

4. Personalized recommendations based on user prefer-

ences and habits

Amazon Alexa: Amazon Alexa is an AI-based personal assistant app that is available on Amazon Echo devices and other smart home devices. Its features include:

1. Voice recognition and natural language processing for hands-free assistance

2. Integration with Amazon services such as Amazon Music, Amazon Prime, and Amazon shopping

3. Ability to set reminders, make phone calls, send messages, and control smart home devices

4. Personalized recommendations based on user preferences and habits

Microsoft Cortana: Microsoft Cortana is an AI-based personal assistant app that is available on Windows devices and other platforms. Its features include:

1. Voice recognition and natural language processing for hands-free assistance

2. Integration with Microsoft services such as Microsoft Office, Microsoft Edge, and Bing

3. Ability to set reminders, make phone calls, send messages, and control smart home devices

4. Personalized recommendations based on user prefer-

ences and habits

These are just a few examples of AI-based personal assistant apps and their features. Each app offers unique capabilities and integrations, and users can choose the one that best fits their needs and preferences.

What is the Potential for AI Assistants in the Future?

The potential for using AI in personal assistant work in the future is vast, and it can make our lives better in many unimaginable ways. If you take everything I listed here and multiply it by ten, that's a good starting point for where we may be with personal assistant AI in a few short years... or even months!

Plus, I'm sure there are several aspects of the job that no one has even considered. Who would have even dreamt 15 years ago that we'd need to focus on social media marketing and self-care for at-home workers as much as we do today?

AI-powered personal assistants have the potential to make our lives more efficient, personalized, accurate, available, and seamless. As AI technology continues to evolve and improve, we can expect to see even more advancements in the field of personal assistant work, leading to greater convenience and quality of life for individuals and businesses alike.

CHAPTER FIVE

AI FOR ARTISTS

One of the most prevalent issues concerning AI today is the creation of imagery known as AI art. Applications like DALL-E 2, Midjourney, Stable Diffusion, and a boatload of others are revolutionizing how we see modern art. With a few simple lines of text, users are able to create absolutely breathtaking images that range from abstract to photorealistic in just a matter of seconds.

While AI is peppered throughout several different industries, AI art has become a hot topic for the general public because it puts a solid visual to this entire phenomenon. People who have never picked up a set of oil paints can make something that they never imagined would be out of their heads and onto a computer screen.

AI art has become a bit of a scapegoat for those who are afraid of AI's growth, but that's normal for something this new that's growing so quickly.

The fact is, AI-generated art can help businesses with so much these days from custom marketing images to product design to data visualization, and even logos. I used Midjourney for the black-and-white illustrations you see at the beginning of each chapter because I wanted to showcase AI's versatility, and I need

How Does AI Create Art?

AI can mimic creativity by using a technique called "generative art." Generative art is a type of algorithm that uses complex mathematical equations to generate images, music, and other creative works.

AI algorithms can be trained on large datasets of existing images, and then use this data to generate new images that are similar in style or content to the original images. This process is called "machine learning" and it involves the algorithm analyzing patterns and features in the data in order to create new images.

For example, an AI algorithm may be trained on a dataset of paintings by a specific artist, and then use this data to generate new paintings that resemble the style of the original artist. The AI algorithm may analyze factors such as color palette, brush stroke patterns, and composition in order to create new images that are similar in style to the original paintings.

The images created by AI algorithms are usually based on existing images that the algorithm has been trained on, but in some cases, these algorithms can also create entirely new images that are not based on any existing data.

Examples of AI's Impact on Art

Way back in the relatively ancient times of 2016, a team of data scientists and art historians used machine learning algorithms to create a new painting in the style of Rembrandt. The painting, titled "The Next Rembrandt," was created by analyzing Rembrandt's existing paintings and using this data to generate a new painting that was similar in style and content. This project demonstrated the potential of AI to create new works of art in the style of historical masters.

In 2015, Google released a project called DeepDream that used machine learning algorithms to generate psychedelic images from existing photos. This project generated a lot of interest and sparked new discussions around the intersection of art and technology.

Rutgers University developed an AI-generated art project called AICAN that uses machine learning algorithms to create new artworks. The project has generated a lot of interest in the art world and has been exhibited in galleries around the world.

In September of 2022, video game designer Jason Allen submitted a work entitled "Théâtre D'opéra Spatial" to the Colorado State Fair's art exhibition. Judges awarded him $300 for what appeared to be a painting straight out of the Renaissance. The only catch was that Allen's work was made with Midjourney, a program that was still very new and relatively unknown in September of 2022.

When Allen revealed on social media that his art was made with AI, the internet exploded. The topic of AI ethics was debated and the general consensus was that he should give the money back and be completely ashamed of himself for not telling the judges about the origins of the work.

The problem with that is there are no laws against what Allen did, and he says he did tell the judges that his work was made with Midjourney. Did they understand what Midjourney was? They say they did not, but the awareness that developed from that debacle opened the path for future art competitions to be on the lookout for similar submissions.

The impact of AI-generated art is still being explored every day, but it has the potential to challenge our traditional notions of creativity and authorship. AI-generated art can also serve as a tool for artists and designers to explore new ideas and techniques. Additionally, AI-generated art has the potential to democratize the art world by making it more accessible to a wider range of people.

How Do These Applications Work?

The individual AI art programs vary quite a bit in their execution, but the concept is relatively similar. While most AI art applications use a simple text prompt as the input, some also use video clips, other images, and even voice commands to work.

I won't go into the step-by-step process for making these applications work, mainly because that information could become obsolete at any time, but I will give a general description of how the most popular programs work.

Midjourney

Midjourney is the de facto art generation program (in 2023) thanks to its ease of use and superior results. Of course, that's completely my opinion, but it has certainly been the gateway drug for those who are not so technology-minded.

To create an image in Midjourney, you must also make an account on Discord, which is essentially a replacement for the forums of old. I won't get into the minute details of creating a Discord account or a Midjourney account, but just realize that you'll need to go through Discord to use Midjourney.

Once everything is set up, you can experiment with text-to-image generation in the various beginner rooms in the Midjourney Discord. Simply use the "/imagine" command in the text input window and fire off your best description for the image you hope to create. Make sure your text includes your subject matter, the environment in which your subject resides, and even the medium and art style you wish to mimic.

Now this is a very basic explanation of how Midjourney works, but there are entire websites and Discord channels dedicated to "promptcrafting," or the art of making the best text prompts for your desired output. It really is a science!

DALL-E 2

OpenAI's DALL-E 2 works as a text-to-image generator, much like Midjourney, but Discord is not required. DALL-E 2 also uses a credit system to charge for your creations, while Midjourney uses a system based on processing hours.

Stable Diffusion

Stable Diffusion, while similar to both Midjourney and DALL-E 2, differs quite a bit in execution. Its code is open source, allowing for much more versatility and expansion. Stable Diffusion can run on your local computer, thanks to its application programming interface (API).

Stability AI, the company behind Stable Diffusion, is even branching out into AI educational models (StableVicuna), code writers (StableLM), and they're the first to release an algorithm that can produce accurate text in an image (DeepFloyd IF).

Free Models

There are also several free alternatives to the above apps, but the quality isn't quite there. Some products, like BlueWillow, act as an aggregator to pull from many of these top models.It's a free app with an improved pay version for more goodies.

Other free text-to-image generators include StarryAI, Nightcafe, Craiyon, Dream by WOMBO, and DeepAI.

How Can Traditional Artists Work Together with AI?

The integration of AI with the traditional art world has opened up new possibilities for collaboration between professional artists and AI. While many have publicly resisted or spoken out against AI art, some have embraced it as a tool.

Using AI as a Tool

Traditional artists can use AI as a tool to enhance their creative process. They can use AI algorithms to generate new ideas or to assist in the creation of complex designs, which the artist can then use as a starting point for their work. Quite honestly, this is something that top artists have done for years, but with stock images and the use of photobashing.

Let's say an artist used an AI-powered tool to generate abstract patterns, textures, or color combinations to incorporate into a painting or sculpture. This approach can help artists explore new styles, techniques, and materials that they might not have considered before.

Additionally, AI can help artists automate certain tasks or processes, such as image editing, color correction, or 3D modeling. This can free up more time for the artist to focus on the creative aspects of their work and experiment with new ideas.

Combining AI-Generated Elements with Traditional Art

Professional artists can also incorporate AI-generated elements into their artwork to create unique pieces that blend traditional and modern techniques. Examples include:

1. Integrating AI-generated patterns or textures into their artwork, such as using AI-generated digital textures as a background for a painting, or incorporating AI-generated patterns into a textile design.

2. Using AI to generate variations of their artwork, such as creating a series of digital images with slightly different color palettes, textures, or compositions.

3. Creating interactive art installations that use AI algorithms to analyze and respond to input from the au-

·dience, such as generating different visual effects based on the movement or sound in the room.

4. Combining physical and digital media to create hybrid artworks, such as creating a sculpture that incorporates both traditional materials and digital projections.

5. Using AI algorithms to analyze their own art and provide feedback on areas for improvement or new directions to explore.

6. Collaborating with AI programmers or data scientists to create generative art, such as creating a system that generates new artwork based on specific parameters or inputs.

The integration of AI into the traditional art world has created new opportunities for collaboration and experimentation. Traditional artists can use AI as a tool to enhance their creative process and create new and exciting works of art without feeling like the AI is doing all the work while the artist takes the credit.

Chapter Six

AI for Writers

A I can be used in various ways to help writers with their work, from generating ideas to editing and proofreading. As I mentioned earlier in this book's introduction, I used ChatGPT to help me plot out the key points of this book. I also used it to help expand a few paragraphs that I felt needed some filling out.

This is truly where a chatbot like ChapGPT shines. As a writer, you're not looking to have AI write for you because the limitations of AI make it fairly obvious. But you are looking to utilize its efficiency as a writing tool. And what better way to prove the point of this chapter than to show the technology in action. Can you tell which paragraphs were "improved" with AI?

Generating Ideas

AI algorithms can help writers generate ideas for their written essays by analyzing data and suggesting topics and themes that may be relevant or interesting. This can involve using natural language processing (NLP) techniques to analyze text and identify patterns and trends.

AI can also improve overall writing skills and streamline the writer's entire creative process. AI can analyze vast amounts of data and identify topics that are relevant to the writer's interests and target audience. This analysis can help the writer come up with new ideas that are fresh, unique, and engaging.

So how does this work, and does it involve plagiarism? No, not technically, as the AI will create a new tone and wording of what it finds out in the vastness of the internet to make its own thing.

And it's important to note that when I say that AI is taking bits and pieces of other work out there to create a new work, it's not stealing large chunks; it's learning from the tone and expression of millions of articles, blog posts, and other written content to identify popular topics, trends, and keywords. By identifying these patterns, AI can help writers discover new topics and themes to explore in their writing, without copying word for word.

And as far as plagiarism goes, most quality AI writing programs, like Jasper or Writecream, will incorporate a plagiarism checker to make sure its tools are not causing problems. The whole plagiarism debate is a common misconception with both AI writing and AI art, but the technology is improving away from the older models that were more obvious in their acquisitions.

NLP-powered tools excel at analyzing written content and providing suggestions for how to improve the writer's style, structure, and tone. By providing feedback and recommendations, these tools can help writers refine their ideas and make their writing more engaging and impactful.

AI-powered brainstorming tools can also generate new ideas based on the writer's interests and preferences. These tools can analyze the writer's past work, social media activity, and other online data to identify topics and themes that the writer is interested in. Based on this analysis, the AI-powered brainstorming tool can generate a list of new ideas that are tailored to the writer's interests and target audience.

Character and Plot Development

There are already tools in place that can help writers create more complex and nuanced characters and develop compelling storylines that resonate with readers. By analyzing vast amounts of data, AI can identify patterns, trends, and themes that can help writers develop characters and plots that are engaging, authentic, and impactful.

One way that AI can assist writers with character development is by analyzing existing characters in literature and media. AI algorithms can analyze vast amounts of data on fictional characters, such as their personalities, motivations, and relationships. This analysis can help writers develop more complex and realistic characters by identifying common traits and archetypes that resonate with readers.

Mimicking tropes has always been a thing with writing, especially with fiction writing, and AI learns from those common patterns. Some AI writing generators (like Jasper, for example) even have sliders and other input that allows you to change the tone and voice of your writing on the fly.

AI can also help writers create characters that are unique and compelling. By analyzing data on real people, such as their personality traits, interests, and behaviors, AI algorithms can help writers develop characters that feel authentic and relatable. AI-powered tools can even generate character profiles based on the writer's input, such as a character's background, personality, and motivations.

In terms of plot development, AI can assist writers by analyzing existing stories and identifying common plot structures and themes. AI algorithms can analyze vast amounts of data on literature, film, and other media to identify common plot elements, such as conflict, resolution, and character arcs. This analysis can help writers develop compelling storylines that follow proven structures and resonate with readers.

AI can also generate new plot ideas based on the writer's input. By analyzing data on existing plots, such as their themes, settings, and characters, AI-powered tools can suggest new plot ideas that are tailored to the writer's interests and target audience.

Language Generation

Natural language processing (NLP) can analyze written content and provide suggestions for how to improve the writer's style, structure, and tone. By providing feedback and recommendations, these tools can help writers refine their language and make their writing more engaging and impactful.

These tools can also identify grammatical errors, suggest corrections, and even rephrase sentences to improve their readability and flow. By catching errors and offering suggestions for improvement, these tools can help writers produce language that is more grammatically correct and easier to read.

But what if you want to completely generate the language with minimal input? AI can generate sentences, paragraphs, and even entire documents based on what you feed it. These tools can generate language that is tailored to the writer's needs, such as summaries, headlines, and marketing copy.

Content Optimization

If you want your written content to reach the biggest audience, AI can assist you with content optimization through keyword analysis. AI-powered tools can analyze search engine data to identify the most popular and relevant keywords and phrases for a given topic or industry. By incorporating these keywords into their content, writers can increase the visibility of their content in search engine results pages (SERPs), driving more traffic to their website or blog.

AI can also assist writers with social media optimization (SMO) by analyzing data on audience engagement. These algorithms can also help writers identify the types of content that are most popular and engaging on social media platforms. By tailoring their content to these trends, writers can increase their social media engagement, driving more traffic to their website or blog.

How about your audience? AI-powered tools can analyze audience data, such as demographics, interests, and behavior, to help writers tailor their content to their target audience. By understanding their audience's preferences and needs, writers can create content that is more relevant and engaging, increasing their impact and reach.

As far as the nitty-gritty formatting and structure, AI can utilize data on user behavior to help writers create more user-friendly and engaging content, which may involve using shorter paragraphs, incorporating bullet points, and adding images. By optimizing the format and structure of their content, writers can potentially enhance user engagement and increase the amount of time visitors spend on their website or blog.

Translation

Language translation can easily be handled with AI as it analyzes text or audio in one language and generates text or audio in another language. This helps writers produce content that is accessible to a wider audience, which can be especially useful for writers who work in multilingual environments, such as international businesses and media outlets.

NLP, machine learning algorithms, and neural networks can easily assist writers in translating content between languages to accurately and efficiently translate text. These tools can help writers communicate with a global audience, expanding their reach and impact.

How does NLP work in this instance? AI-powered translation tools can analyze the context and structure of the source language and use algorithms to generate translations that are accurate and contextually appropriate. AI-powered translation tools with NLP can better understand the nuances of language and produce translations that are more natural and fluent.

With machine learning algorithms, language AI can be trained on vast amounts of data to improve the accuracy of translations over time. By continually learning from new data, AI-powered translation tools can adapt to changing language trends and produce more accurate translations. This is especially important as generational speech changes on a regular basis.

On a similar scale, neural networks can be used to identify patterns in language and generate translations that are more natural and fluent. Neural networks in the AI algorithms can produce translations that are more similar to human-generated translations, increasing their accuracy and readability.

AI-powered translation tools can also assist writers with translation speed. By automating the translation process, these tools can translate large amounts of text in a fraction of the time it would take a human translator. This can be especially useful for writers who need to produce content in multiple languages quickly, such as journalists or content marketers.

Researching and Gathering Information

AI can be used to help writers research and gather information by providing them with quick and easy access to relevant and reliable sources. These tools can analyze vast amounts of data from websites, academic papers, and news articles, to identify key information related to a specific topic.

AI can also help writers to organize their research by categorizing and summarizing information, which can save them time and effort. Additionally, AI can generate content based on a given set of criteria, which can be useful for generating ideas, creating outlines, or even writing drafts.

Writing Assistance

AI can be used to assist writers with the actual writing process in various ways. Grammar checkers, spell-checkers, and language suggestion tools can analyze the writer's text and provide suggestions for improvements, such as correcting grammatical errors, improving sentence structure, and suggesting alternative word choices.

AI can also be used to provide feedback on the quality of the writing, such as the clarity, coherence, and overall readability. AI-powered tools can analyze the writer's text and provide feedback on the use of passive voice, sentence complexity, and other factors that may affect the readability of the content. We've been seeing this for years in programs like Grammarly or even the built-in service in Microsoft Word, but the nuances of the English language are becoming no match for this AI as it grows and learns.

One way I personally use AI in this context is to improve a piece that I've already written. I'll feed a few paragraphs through GPT-4 or Jasper and watch as it rephrases my words with that added boost that I didn't even know I needed, all while preserving the integrity of the original writing. Even at that point, I don't use the AI output verbatim, but it's good to have those suggested edits as if AI were my very own writing partner.

Editing and Proofreading

AI algorithms can also be used to edit and proofread written essays. This can involve using NLP techniques to identify grammar and spelling errors, as well as suggesting alternative wording for unclear or awkward sentences.

AI algorithms can use NLP techniques to identify relevant keywords and topics, and can also analyze patterns and trends in the data to identify new ideas and insights.

There's no doubt that AI can be a powerful tool for writers by providing assistance throughout the entire writing process. By using AI to generate ideas, gather information, and edit and proofread their work, writers can produce high-quality written essays that are accurate, engaging, and well-written.

How Can AI Help Copywriters and Editors?

Outside of the scope of writing in general, AI can be a helpful tool for both copywriters and editors in various ways. Here are some examples:

Generating Headlines and Titles

AI can help copywriters generate headlines and titles by using NLP and machine learning algorithms to analyze existing headlines and identify patterns and trends that are likely to be successful.

For example, an AI-powered tool may analyze a large dataset of headlines and identify common structures or phrasing that tend to be effective in attracting readers' attention. The tool may also analyze the emotional tone of headlines and identify which emotions are most likely to resonate with readers.

AI can also generate headlines and titles automatically, based on a set of criteria provided by the copywriter. For instance, a copywriter can input a topic or a set of keywords, and an AI-powered tool can generate several headline options based on those inputs.

Moreover, AI can test different headlines and titles to determine which ones are most effective. The tool can analyze the click-through rates or engagement metrics of each headline and adjust the headline based on the performance data. This can help copywriters optimize their headlines for maximum impact and engagement.

While AI can be a useful tool for copywriters to generate headlines and titles that are effective and engaging, it's important to note that AI-generated headlines should be reviewed and edited by humans to ensure they align with the brand's voice and messaging.

Improving Writing Quality

AI-powered writing tools can check the grammar, spelling, and punctuation of a writer's text, helping to ensure that it is error-free and easy to read. This can be especially helpful for writers who are not native English speakers or who struggle with grammar and spelling.

Of course, this isn't an exact science right out of the box, but AI's learning capabilities help out a lot in this instance. If you're writing (or editing) a sci-fi novel that's loaded with made-up alien names, you can assign the AI to ignore or add those words to its own glossary for future use.

AI models can also provide suggestions for improving the clarity and readability of the writing, such as rephrasing a sentence to make it more concise or breaking up a long paragraph into smaller chunks for easier reading.

The tone and style of the writing is also important to stay consistent with the intended audience and brand voice. The AI tool may suggest using more formal language for a business report or a more conversational tone for a blog post.

As far as the overall coherence and structure of the writing, AI can highlight areas that may need further development or refinement. This can help writers identify areas where they can improve their writing skills and ultimately produce higher quality content.

And if it's fresh ideas and concept inspiration that you're after, AI may analyze existing content and suggest new topics or angles that have not been explored before.

Identifying Plagiarism

AI can help identify plagiarism in writing by comparing a given text with a large database of other texts, including previously published works and academic papers.

There are even several different types of plagiarism that can be detected by AI, such as verbatim plagiarism (word-for-word copying), paraphrasing plagiarism (rewriting a text in one's own words), and mosaic plagiarism (combining different sources without proper citation).

AI-powered plagiarism detection tools can also check for unintentional plagiarism, such as accidental copying of text due to poor paraphrasing skills or inadequate citation practices. The tool can flag instances where a writer may have inadvertently used language or ideas from another source without proper attribution.

Oftentimes, writers can inadvertently copy themselves in a repeated pattern that may not be apparent at the time of writing, but AI can help identify this self-plagiarism, too. AI-powered tools can compare a writer's current text with their previous work and identify instances where there is overlap or reuse of material.

What Are Some Examples of AI Writing and its Impact on the Modern World?

AI-generated writing is becoming increasingly common, and its impact is being felt across a wide range of industries. Here are some examples of AI-generated writing and its impact:

News articles

AI can be a useful tool for writers to create news articles in several ways:

1. Content generation: AI can be used to generate content based on a specific topic or keyword. For example, a writer can input a topic such as "climate change" into an AI platform, and the platform can generate a news article with the latest statistics and developments on the topic. This can save writers time and effort in researching and writing the article.

2. Fact-checking: AI can be used to fact-check news articles, ensuring that the information presented is accurate and up-to-date. This can help writers avoid errors and misinformation in their articles.

3. Language assistance: AI can be used to assist writers in creating engaging and well-written articles. For example, an AI platform can suggest synonyms or alternative phrasing to help writers avoid repeating the same words or phrases throughout the article.

4. Personalization: AI can help writers personalize their articles based on the reader's interests or preferences. For example, an AI platform can analyze a reader's

reading history and suggest related articles that the reader may find interesting.

Product Descriptions

AI algorithms are being used to generate product descriptions for online retailers. This can help retailers create unique and engaging descriptions for their products, without the need for human writers to spend hours researching and writing.

1. Data analysis: AI can analyze data such as customer reviews, product specifications, and competitor descriptions to identify the most important features and benefits of the product. This analysis can help the AI generate a comprehensive and accurate description of the product.

2. Personalization: AI can personalize product descriptions based on the customer's interests, preferences, and buying history. So if a customer frequently buys products with a particular feature, the AI can highlight that feature in the product description.

3. Tone and style: AI can analyze the tone and style of the product description and adapt it to the target audience. With a product aimed at a younger audience, the AI can use more casual language and incorporate

trendy phrases.

4. Optimization: AI can optimize product descriptions for search engines by incorporating keywords and phrases that potential customers are likely to use when searching for the product.

Legal documents

AI algorithms are being used to generate legal documents, such as contracts and briefs. This can save lawyers and law firms time and money, and can also help ensure that legal documents are accurate and consistent.

1. Template creation: AI can create templates for legal documents based on the specific legal requirements and regulations of a particular jurisdiction. These templates can be customized for individual clients, saving time and effort for lawyers and legal professionals.

2. Data analysis: AI can analyze vast amounts of legal data, including case law, statutes, and regulations, to identify relevant legal clauses and provisions to include in a legal document. This analysis can help ensure that the document is comprehensive and accurate.

3. Contract review: AI can review contracts and identify any discrepancies or inconsistencies, helping legal pro-

fessionals to avoid potential errors or misunderstandings.

4. Natural language generation: AI can generate legal documents using natural language processing techniques to ensure that the language is clear and easy to understand for clients and other parties involved in the legal transaction.

Chatbots

AI algorithms are being used to generate written responses for chatbots and virtual assistants. This can help companies provide faster and more efficient customer service, and can also help them scale their customer support operations without needing to hire additional staff.

A chatbot is a computer program designed to simulate human conversation through text or voice interactions. Chatbots use AI and NLP technologies to understand and interpret user input, provide responses, and carry out automated tasks.

Here's how a chatbot typically works:

1. User input: The user initiates a conversation with the chatbot by typing a message or speaking a command.

2. NLP processing: The chatbot uses NLP algorithms to analyze the user's input and identify the intent behind

the message.

3. Response generation: Based on the user's intent, the chatbot generates a response using pre-written text, machine learning algorithms, or a combination of both.

4. Action execution: If the chatbot is designed to carry out automated tasks, it may execute actions such as placing an order, scheduling an appointment, or providing information.

5. Repeat: The conversation continues in a back-and-forth exchange between the user and the chatbot, with the chatbot interpreting each new message and generating an appropriate response.

Chatbots can be integrated into various platforms such as websites, messaging apps, and voice assistants. They can be designed for various purposes such as customer service, sales, marketing, and personal assistance. Chatbots can save time and resources for businesses by providing instant responses to frequently asked questions and handling simple tasks, while also providing a more personalized and interactive user experience.

Creative Writing

AI algorithms are even being used to generate creative writing, such as poetry and short stories. While some writers may view this as a threat to their livelihoods, others see it as a way to augment their own creative processes and generate new ideas.

AI can generate creative writing projects by using machine learning algorithms and NLP techniques to analyze and understand patterns in creative writing. Here are some ways AI can help in generating creative writing projects:

1. Idea generation: AI can generate ideas for creative writing projects based on specific topics or themes. So if a writer is looking for inspiration for a science fiction story, an AI platform can suggest various concepts and plotlines based on analysis of existing science fiction works.

2. Language assistance: AI can suggest alternative phrasing, synonyms, and even generate sentences or paragraphs based on the writer's writing style. For instance, an AI platform can analyze a person's writing style and suggest ways to improve sentence structure, tone, and pacing.

3. Style imitation: AI can analyze an author's writing style and generate new content that imitates that style. If you're looking for a short story in the style of Hemingway, Poe, or any other famous author, AI can do that.

4. Personalization: AI can personalize creative writing projects based on the writer's preferences and interests. An AI platform can suggest storylines or characters that are more likely to resonate with the writer's audience or reader demographic.

The impact of AI-generated writing is still being studied and debated, with some arguing that it will revolutionize the way we produce and consume written content, while others fear that it will replace human writers altogether. However, it is clear that AI-generated writing is already having a significant impact on various industries, and it is likely to become even more prevalent in the future.

The potential for collaboration between writers and AI is vast. By working together, writers and AI can help each other produce better quality work, save time and increase efficiency, and reach wider audiences. That said, writers should still be the ones in control of their work, with AI serving as a helpful assistant.

Chapter Seven

AI for Musicians

A common sticking point for those of us old folks who can't understand the appeal of new music is the (over)use of auto-tuning software to change the tone and pitch of a singer's voice to match the music. This has been going for several years, and is actually considered an early version of AI enhancement for musicians.

But vocal synthesis technology is only one of the many ways in which AI can be used in the music industry.

Music Composition

AI can be used to compose music, either by generating entirely new music from scratch or by analyzing existing music and using that analysis to generate new music.

The AI system can be trained on a large dataset of music using machine learning techniques such as neural networks, deep learning, and reinforcement learning. The system can analyze the patterns and structures in the music, learn from them, and then use this knowledge to create its own compositions.

One popular approach to generative music is to use a technique called "neural style transfer," where a machine learning algorithm is used to extract the style and structure of a particular piece of music, and then apply these characteristics to a new composition. This technique has already been used to generate music in a variety of genres, from classical to electronic music.

Another approach to generative music is to use evolutionary algorithms, which mimic the process of natural selection to generate new music. In this approach, the system creates a population of musical sequences, which are then evaluated based on a set of criteria such as melodic complexity, harmonic consistency, and rhythmic interest. The best sequences are then "selected" and used as the basis for the next generation, with mutations and variations introduced to create new compositions.

In both cases, the AI system is able to generate new musical compositions that are similar in style to existing music, but also have unique qualities and characteristics that make them original.

Music Production

AI can also be used to assist with music production tasks, such as mixing and mastering. Some AI systems can analyze audio tracks and automatically adjust levels and EQ settings to create a more polished and professional sound.

Another way that AI can be used to produce music is by using it to control digital instruments and sound effects. For example, some music software and hardware systems use AI algorithms to manipulate the sound of a guitar or synthesizer, creating new sounds and textures that would be difficult or impossible to achieve manually.

Vocal Synthesis

Here it is, the big autotune debate. While the resulting sound of auto-tuning software has been obvious and robotic in the past, recent improvements make its use almost undetectable.

AI can be used to create realistic vocal synthesizers, which can be used to create new vocal performances or to mimic the voice of a particular singer. For example, some AI systems can analyze a singer's voice and create a digital model of their vocal characteristics, which can then be used to synthesize new vocal performances. While this is impressive, copying a singer's voice is still very much against copyright law.

It's also important to note that AI voice synthesis and auto-tune are two different technologies that are used for different purposes.

AI voice synthesis refers to the use of artificial intelligence and machine learning to create a synthesized voice that sounds like a human voice. This technology is used in applications such as text-to-speech (TTS) systems and virtual assistants, where the goal is to create a natural-sounding voice that can speak various languages and dialects. AI voice synthesis algorithms analyze and model human speech patterns, intonation, and prosody to create a synthesized voice that sounds like a real person.

Autotune, on the other hand, is a pitch correction software that is used in music production to correct pitch inaccuracies in a singer's voice. Autotune algorithms analyze the pitch of a singer's voice and adjust it in real-time to match the desired pitch, creating a smoother and more polished sound. This technology is used in genres such as pop, hip-hop, and electronic music to achieve a specific sound and style.

While both AI voice synthesis and autotune use algorithms to modify sound, they serve different purposes. AI voice synthesis creates a synthesized voice that sounds like a real person, while autotune corrects pitch inaccuracies in a singer's voice to create a polished sound in music production.

Lyric Generation

AI can also be used to generate lyrics for songs. Some AI systems use natural language processing algorithms to analyze large datasets of existing lyrics and generate new lyrics that are similar in style and theme.

To make poems or song lyrics rhyme, AI algorithms use a combination of phonetic analysis and pattern recognition to identify words that sound similar and can be used to create a rhyme scheme. The algorithm can also use different types of rhymes, such as perfect rhymes, slant rhymes, and eye rhymes, to create a more varied and interesting rhyme scheme.

So how does this work? First, AI algorithms are trained on a large dataset of existing lyrics and poems to learn the patterns and structures of language used in songwriting and poetry.

Then, the AI algorithms use NLP techniques to analyze the text and identify patterns such as rhyme schemes, syllable counts, and word associations. Based on the learned patterns and structures, the AI algorithm generates new lyrics or poetry that follow the same style, rhythm, and rhyme scheme as the input dataset.

From there, the AI-generated lyrics or poetry are reviewed and edited by humans to ensure that they make sense and convey the intended message.

Can AI Actually Write Musical Notes?

AI can read and write musical notes using machine learning algorithms that can analyze and process musical data, such as sheet music or audio recordings.

The AI algorithm is fed with musical data, such as sheet music, MIDI files, or audio recordings. The AI algorithm then uses machine learning techniques, such as deep neural networks, to analyze and process the musical data. This involves breaking down the musical data into its constituent parts, such as individual notes, chords, and rhythms.

The new music is created based on the patterns and structures identified in the analyzed data. This involves using generative models that can create new musical phrases, melodies, and harmonies.

Music can also be transcribed from audio recordings into sheet music or MIDI files. This involves using signal processing techniques to identify the individual notes and rhythms in the audio recording and converting them into a digital format.

The AI algorithm can also be used to compose music by generating new musical phrases, melodies, and harmonies that are stylistically similar to existing music. This involves using machine learning models that can learn the characteristics and structures of different musical genres and styles.

It's worth noting that while AI can be used to assist with these tasks, it is still up to the human musician to curate and refine the output. AI can help generate ideas and inspiration, but ultimately the musician is the one who decides which ideas to keep and which to discard.

How Can AI Help Protect Musicians?

AI can help musicians and songwriters protect their intellectual property by monitoring the internet for copyright infringement and identifying unauthorized use of their music.

This is done through AI-powered Content ID systems that are used by platforms like YouTube, SoundCloud, and other music streaming platforms to automatically detect and identify copyrighted content. These systems work by scanning the audio and video content uploaded to the platform and comparing it to a database of copyrighted content provided by the copyright owner. If the system finds a match, it can flag the content and take action, such as removing it or demonetizing the video.

AI-powered copyright monitoring tools continuously scan the internet for unauthorized use of copyrighted material. They search for matches between copyrighted works and content that is being distributed or used online without permission. This can help copyright owners identify instances of infringement and take action to protect their intellectual property.

AI-powered songwriting assistance tools can also help musicians to create original works that do not infringe on the rights of others. These tools can analyze existing music and provide suggestions for new melodies, chord progressions, and lyrics that are unique and original.

There are also music rights organizations that use AI to manage their catalogs of copyrighted works more efficiently. The AI systems can be used to identify instances of unauthorized use of copyrighted works, and to track and distribute royalties to copyright owners.

It's worth noting that AI is not a substitute for legal advice or human judgment, and copyright owners should still take steps to protect their rights through registration, licensing, and legal action if necessary.

Examples of AI Music Generators

Amper Music

Amper Music is a popular AI music generator that allows users to create original music using artificial intelligence. It offers a simple interface and a wide variety of customizable options, including genre, tempo, and instrumentation.

AIVA

AIVA (Artificial Intelligence Virtual Artist) is an AI music generator that specializes in classical music. It uses deep learning algorithms to analyze and learn from existing compositions, and can generate original pieces in a wide range of styles.

Jukedeck

Jukedeck is an AI music generator that allows users to create custom tracks using a library of pre-made musical elements.

It offers a simple interface and a wide range of customization options, including genre, tempo, and instrumentation.

Amadeus Code

Amadeus Code is an AI music generator that specializes in pop and rock music. It uses machine learning algorithms to analyze existing compositions and generate original pieces in a wide range of styles.

OpenAI MuseNet/Jukebox

OpenAI MuseNet and Jukebox are experimental AI music generators that use machine learning algorithms to generate original pieces in a wide range of styles, from classical to pop. It offers a unique interface and a high level of customization options,but requires some technical knowledge to use.

Chapter Eight

AI for Game Designers

Imagine a video game designer sitting in front of their computer, staring at a blank screen and wondering how to create the next big hit game. Suddenly, an AI-powered assistant pops up on their screen, offering suggestions and ideas for characters, storylines, and gameplay mechanics.

With AI, game designers can use machine learning algorithms to analyze data and predict player behavior, making it easier to create engaging and challenging gameplay experiences. AI can also be used to generate new content, such as game levels, environments, and characters, based on the designer's preferences and specifications.

In addition, AI can help game designers to test and refine their games more quickly and efficiently. For example, AI can be used to simulate thousands of game sessions, identify bugs and glitches in real time, and provide suggestions for improvements. This means that game designers can spend less time testing and more time designing and refining their games, leading to better games and happier players.

It's almost like having a game design genie that can grant wishes and help game designers create amazing games that players will love. So, the next time you're playing your favorite video game, remember that AI may have played a big role in making it fun and addictive!

Let's take a deeper look at some of the more important aspects of game design that can be helped with AI.

Procedural Generation

With AI, video game designers can use procedural content generation techniques to create endless amounts of content for their games, from levels to characters to weapons. By analyzing patterns and structures in existing content, AI can generate new, unique content that fits seamlessly into the game. And the best part? It's all done automatically, so designers can focus on creating the gameplay experience they want, without worrying about the details.

Of course, AI-generated content isn't always perfect. Sometimes the characters look like they were designed by a five-year-old with a crayon, and the levels can be more confusing than a Rubik's cube with half the stickers torn off. But with a little tweaking and fine-tuning, designers can take the AI-generated content and make it their own, creating a game that's both unique and fun to play.

I'm convinced that the ability to create complete, finished games with AI is right around the corner. With the ability to write code, design animations and artwork, and analyze the "perfect player" profile, we're not far from this becoming a reality.

The question is, are players ready for that?

Player Behavior Analysis

You know what they say -- if you want to catch a gamer, you've got to think like a gamer. And that's exactly what AI-powered player behavior analysis does. It thinks like a gamer, analyzes their every move, and helps game designers create the ultimate gaming experience.

With AI, game designers can analyze player behavior in real time, tracking everything from the levels they complete to the weapons they use. This information is then used to create more engaging and challenging gameplay experiences, tailored to each player's unique preferences and play style. So, if you're the type of player who always goes for the shotgun over the pistol, the AI will take note and make sure there are plenty of shotguns in the game for you to blast away.

But AI player behavior analysis isn't just about creating better gameplay -- it's also about keeping players hooked. By analyzing player behavior, AI can identify when players are becoming disengaged or frustrated, and offer suggestions for how to keep them playing. Maybe you're stuck on a particularly difficult level -- the AI might suggest a different strategy, or even offer to give you a boost to get past it. Or maybe you're just getting bored with the game -- the AI might suggest new challenges or rewards to keep you coming back for more.

Of course, there are some downsides to AI player behavior analysis. Some players might feel like they're being watched, or that their every move is being analyzed and scrutinized. But for most gamers, the benefits far outweigh the risks. After all, who doesn't want to play a game that's tailor-made just for them?

Game Balancing

With AI, game designers can analyze the gameplay data to determine which weapons, characters, or abilities are overpowered and which are underpowered. No more endless hours of playtesting and tweaking -- the AI can do it all in a fraction of the time, leaving designers free to indulge in their favorite pastime: caffeine consumption.

AI can even help balance the more subtle aspects of the game, like the pacing and difficulty curve, by analyzing the gameplay data. Maybe the game is too easy in the beginning and too hard at the end. The AI can suggest changes to the levels and enemies to make the difficulty more consistent. Or maybe players are getting bored with the same old objectives so the AI suggests new challenges and objectives to keep things fresh and exciting.

And the best part? With AI balancing, designers can make sure that every player has a chance to succeed, no matter their skill level. So even if you're the type of player who can barely make it past the tutorial level without dying, the AI can make sure there's a difficulty level just for you. Who knows, you might even become the next big esports superstar, all thanks to the power of AI balancing.

AI-Controlled Game Characters

There are oceans of memes about how bad AI-controlled non-player characters (NPCs) can be in many modern games, but the fact is that the technology has come so far in just the last year that having human-like conversations with the town merchant is entirely possible right now.

Of course, in a role-playing scenario, the more realistic the AI, the better the immersion and player experience can be.

How Has Video Game AI Improved Over the Years?

Improved AI Behavior

AI algorithms have become more sophisticated and can now simulate more complex behaviors for NPCs in video games. This includes behaviors such as decision-making, pathfinding, and adaptive learning.

Better Graphics and Animation

AI has enabled video game developers to create more realistic graphics and animations for characters, using techniques such as machine learning-based image processing and motion capture.

Voice Recognition and Natural Language Processing

AI-powered voice recognition and natural language processing (NLP) have enabled video game characters to respond to player commands and engage in more natural and fluid conversations.

Personalization and Adaptability

AI can personalize the gameplay experience for each player by analyzing their preferences and adapting the game's difficulty level and content accordingly. This creates a more engaging and immersive experience for players.

Enhanced Enemy AI

AI algorithms have enabled video game developers to create more intelligent and challenging enemies, such as those that learn from the player's behavior and adapt their tactics accordingly.

Character Customization

AI algorithms can be used to generate custom characters based on player preferences, allowing players to create unique and personalized avatars.

AI has revolutionized the video game industry by enabling more realistic, dynamic, and personalized gameplay experiences. As AI continues to evolve, we can expect even more advancements in video game character development and gameplay.

Can AI Really Write Code?

Game developers and programmers can use the latest AI to create custom algorithms that can generate game code based on pre-defined rules and parameters in a fraction of the time as it took before.

So yes, it can actually write programming language parameters that work. Let's take a look at a few of the programming languages that can be written by AI.

1. Python: Python is a popular language for machine

learning and AI applications, and AI algorithms can generate code in Python for tasks such as data analysis, natural language processing, and computer vision.

2. Java: Java is a versatile language used for a variety of applications, including mobile app development, web development, and enterprise software. AI algorithms can generate code in Java for tasks such as database management and software development.

3. JavaScript: JavaScript is a scripting language used for front-end web development and building interactive user interfaces. AI algorithms can generate code in JavaScript for tasks such as website optimization and dynamic content generation.

4. C++: C++ is a high-performance language used for applications such as gaming, virtual reality, and scientific computing. AI algorithms can generate code in C++ for tasks such as optimization and parallel computing.

5. SQL: SQL is a language used for managing and querying relational databases. AI algorithms can generate code in SQL for tasks such as database management and data analysis.

6. HTML: AI can analyze the requirements of a requested website, including the layout, content, and design,

and use this information to generate HTML code. This code will contain the necessary tags and elements that make up the website's structure, such as headings, paragraphs, images, and links.

Animation and 3D

AI can turn a text prompt into 3D animation using a combination of NLP and computer graphics techniques.

The AI algorithm analyzes the text prompt to identify the key elements, such as characters, objects, and settings.

Based on the analyzed text prompt, the AI algorithm creates a 3D scene with the identified elements. This involves creating 3D models of the characters and objects, and designing the environment and setting of the scene.

The AI algorithm then generates animations for the characters and objects, based on the actions and interactions described in the text prompt. This involves defining the movements, expressions, and behaviors of the characters and objects, and animating them accordingly.

Once the 3D scene and animations have been generated, the AI algorithm renders the final animation as a video file.

Chapter Nine

AI for Healthcare

AI has the potential to revolutionize the healthcare industry by providing new tools and techniques for diagnosis, treatment, and patient care.

One of the most significant benefits of AI in healthcare is that it can help medical professionals provide better and more personalized care to their patients. For example, AI algorithms can analyze large amounts of medical data, such as patient records and medical images, to identify patterns and trends that may not be immediately apparent to a human clinician. This can help doctors diagnose diseases more accurately and develop more effective treatment plans.

AI can also help to reduce medical errors, which are a significant cause of morbidity and mortality in healthcare. AI-powered decision support systems can help doctors make better clinical decisions, reducing the risk of misdiagnosis and medication errors. Additionally, AI-powered robots can assist with surgeries and other procedures, reducing the risk of human error and improving surgical outcomes.

Another way that AI can benefit healthcare workers is by improving the efficiency of healthcare operations. Chatbots can help to streamline patient communication and scheduling, reducing wait times and improving patient satisfaction. Additionally, AI algorithms can analyze healthcare workflows to identify areas where processes could be streamlined, reducing waste and saving time and money.

Finally, AI can help to advance medical research and drug development. AI algorithms can analyze large datasets of genetic and medical information to identify potential targets for drug development, speeding up the drug discovery process. Additionally, AI-powered clinical trials can help to identify patient subgroups that may respond better to certain treatments, improving the effectiveness of medical interventions.

Is AI Safe for Patients Who Need Specialized Care?

While some patients may have concerns about AI in healthcare, it is important to note that AI can help to diagnose diseases more accurately, develop more effective treatment plans, and reduce the risk of medical errors, ultimately improving patient safety and quality of care.

These algorithms must be subject to rigorous ethical and regulatory frameworks to ensure that they do not perpetuate biases or discriminate against certain patient groups. This includes careful selection of data sources, transparency in algorithm development and decision-making, and ongoing monitoring and evaluation of AI systems to identify and address any issues that may arise.

Patients should also be informed and educated about the use of AI in healthcare, including the benefits and potential risks, as well as their rights with respect to the use of their personal data. Patients should have the opportunity to provide informed consent for the use of AI in their care, and to ask questions or express concerns about the use of AI in their treatment.

AI can work safely in a healthcare environment when it is designed and implemented with safety, accuracy, transparency, and ethical considerations in mind. Patients should not fear AI, but rather view it as a tool to improve the quality and safety of their care when used appropriately and in conjunction with human clinicians. By ensuring that AI is subject to rigorous testing, validation, and ethical frameworks, we can maximize its potential to improve patient outcomes and advance healthcare.

Chapter Ten

AI for Finance

AI has the potential to transform the finance industry by providing new tools and techniques for investment analysis, risk management, fraud detection, and customer service. Here is an overview of some of the benefits:

1. Investment analysis: AI algorithms can analyze large amounts of financial data to identify patterns and predict market trends, helping investors make better-informed decisions.

2. Trading algorithms: AI algorithms can create trading algorithms that use machine learning to analyze market data in real-time and make trades based on specific criteria.

3. Risk management: AI algorithms can monitor financial markets and identify potential risks, helping financial institutions to manage their portfolios more effectively.

4. Fraud detection: AI algorithms can analyze financial transactions to detect fraudulent activity and alert financial institutions to potential issues.

5. Customer service: AI-powered chatbots can assist customers with common queries, such as account balances, transaction history, and investment advice.

6. Credit scoring: AI algorithms can analyze credit histories and other financial data to assess creditworthiness and make lending decisions.

7. Compliance monitoring: AI algorithms can monitor financial transactions for compliance with regulatory requirements, helping financial institutions to avoid penalties and fines.

8. Anti-money laundering (AML): AI algorithms can analyze financial transactions to detect and prevent money laundering activities.

Should We Trust AI with Our Money?

Letting machines handle our money is a touchy subject and ultimately up to the individual, but there are certainly benefits to AI's involvement in money management.

One of the primary benefits of AI in finance is its ability to improve risk management. AI algorithms can analyze historical financial data and market trends to identify potential risks and predict future market movements, allowing financial institutions to make more informed investment decisions and reduce their exposure to risk.

AI can also help to automate many manual financial processes, such as underwriting loans and processing insurance claims, reducing the time and resources required for these tasks. Additionally, AI-powered chatbots can improve customer service by providing instant answers to common customer queries and streamlining customer interactions.

Another area where AI can benefit the finance industry is in fraud detection and prevention. AI algorithms can analyze large amounts of transaction data to identify patterns and anomalies that may indicate fraudulent activity. By identifying and flagging potential instances of fraud in real-time, financial institutions can minimize their losses and reduce the risk of financial crime.

AI can also be used to develop more accurate credit scoring models, which can help to increase access to credit for underserved populations. By using non-traditional data sources, such as social media activity and mobile phone usage, AI algorithms can provide a more comprehensive view of an individual's creditworthiness, allowing financial institutions to make more informed lending decisions.

Finally, AI can be used to improve investment management by providing personalized investment advice and portfolio management services. An individual's financial goals, risk tolerance, and investment preferences are all factors that AI algorithms can use to develop customized investment strategies that meet their specific needs. This can help individuals to make more informed investment decisions and achieve their financial goals more effectively.

AI has the potential to transform the finance industry in numerous ways, but as financial institutions continue to explore the potential of AI, we can expect to see even more innovation and disruption in the years ahead.

AI and the Stock Market

AI can be used with the stock market in various ways to analyze data, make predictions, and inform trading decisions. While turning your entire investment portfolio over to AI is probably not something that most people would be comfortable with, you might be surprised at how many large investment firms already offer AI-powered investment tracking and guidance.

If you're a broker looking to utilize AI, there are several ways this can be achieved.

As with most other industries involved with AI, the algorithms are used to analyze vast amounts of financial data, such as market trends, news articles, and social media activity, to identify patterns and insights that humans may miss. This can help investors make more informed decisions and stay ahead of market trends.

The AI can build predictive models that forecast market trends and identify potential risks and opportunities. This can help investors make more accurate predictions about the performance of individual stocks, sectors, and the overall market.

These tools can also be used to develop and execute trading strategies based on market data and predictive models. This includes automated trading algorithms that can buy and sell stocks based on predefined rules or based on real-time market data.

Of course, there's always the issue of risk with anything as serious as investing and financial planning. Luckily, AI algorithms can help investors manage risk by analyzing portfolios, identifying potential risks, and suggesting changes to minimize risk exposure.

Social media and news articles can be analyzed by the AI to gauge market sentiment and identify trends that may impact stock prices, while AI algorithms can be used to detect fraudulent activity in the stock market, such as insider trading or market manipulation.

Chapter Eleven

AI for Education

New tools and techniques for personalized learning, student assessment, and administrative tasks are key in AI's role in education, but it's also a very delicate subject. Many parents, rightfully so, are concerned about AI teaching their children. That said, here are some ways AI can assist in the education sector:

1. Personalized learning: AI algorithms can analyze student data, such as learning styles and academic performance, to provide personalized learning recommendations and feedback.

2. Intelligent tutoring systems: AI-powered tutoring systems can provide students with personalized support and feedback, helping them to better understand and retain information.

3. Adaptive assessments: AI algorithms can provide adaptive assessments that adjust the difficulty of questions based on a student's responses, providing a more

accurate assessment of their knowledge.

4. Administrative tasks: AI-powered systems can assist with administrative tasks, such as grading, scheduling, and resource allocation, reducing the workload for educators.

5. Language learning: AI algorithms can provide personalized language learning recommendations and feedback, helping students to improve their language skills.

6. Virtual classrooms: AI-powered virtual classrooms can provide remote learning opportunities, enabling students to learn from anywhere in the world.

7. Learning analytics: AI algorithms can analyze student data to identify patterns and predict student outcomes, helping educators to better understand student needs and improve their teaching strategies.

8. Accessibility: AI-powered technologies can improve accessibility for students with disabilities, such as providing text-to-speech functionality for students with visual impairments.

AI can act as a teacher in a variety of ways, from intelligent tutoring systems that provide personalized instruction to chatbots that can answer student questions and provide support outside of the classroom.

While some parents may have concerns about the use of AI in education, it is important to note that AI is not intended to replace human teachers but rather to support and augment their abilities. AI can help to identify individual student needs and provide targeted support and feedback, freeing up teachers to focus on other aspects of teaching and learning. AI can also help to address issues of equity and access by providing personalized learning opportunities to students who may not have access to traditional classroom resources or support.

However, it is important to ensure that AI is used appropriately and ethically in educational settings. AI algorithms must be transparent, accurate, and unbiased, and they must comply with data privacy regulations to protect student data. Additionally, AI should be used to supplement and enhance teacher-led instruction, rather than replacing it entirely.

Parents should be informed and educated about the use of AI in their child's education, including the benefits and potential risks, as well as their rights with respect to the use of their child's personal data. Parents should have the opportunity to provide informed consent for the use of AI in their child's education and to ask questions or express concerns about the use of AI in their child's learning experience.

AI can act as a valuable teacher in an educational environment when used appropriately and in conjunction with human teachers. By providing personalized learning experiences, feedback, and support, AI can help to improve student outcomes and address issues of equity and access. However, it is important to ensure that AI is used ethically and transparently, and that parents are informed and educated about the use of AI in their child's education. The use of AI in education should ultimately be guided by a commitment to improving student learning and outcomes while respecting student privacy and well-being.

How AI Can Help with Adult Learning?

With the increasing availability of online courses and resources, adults can access a wealth of information and knowledge from the comfort of their own homes. AI can play a valuable role in this learning process by helping to personalize the learning experience, providing feedback, and improving retention.

One way adults can use AI to learn at home is through adaptive learning. Adaptive learning systems use machine learning algorithms to personalize the learning experience based on individual needs and abilities. These systems analyze the learner's performance, identify areas of weakness, and adjust the content and difficulty level accordingly. This approach can help learners to stay engaged and motivated, as they are presented with content that is challenging but not overwhelming.

Another area where AI can be particularly useful is in language learning. AI-powered language learning platforms can provide personalized feedback on pronunciation, grammar, and vocabulary, allowing learners to improve their skills more quickly and effectively. These systems can also adapt to the learner's individual pace and style of learning, making the process more engaging and efficient.

AI can also be used to teach complex concepts in fields such as mathematics and science to help further current education or job update requirements. By providing interactive simulations and visualizations, AI-powered educational tools can help learners to understand difficult concepts in a more intuitive way. AI can also help to identify and correct misconceptions, providing immediate feedback and preventing learners from developing incorrect understandings.

Overall, AI is best at teaching subjects that are data-driven and objective, such as mathematics and science, where it can provide personalized feedback and adapt to the learner's individual needs.

Chapter Twelve

AI for the Transportation Industry

AI has the potential to transform the transportation industry by providing new tools and techniques for efficiency, safety, and sustainability. Let's take a look at a few concepts that are in place today.

Vehicle Maintenance

To start, the issue of vehicle maintenance is a big one, especially in fleet situations. AI algorithms can analyze data from sensors and other sources to predict when maintenance is needed on vehicles and infrastructure, reducing downtime and improving safety.

This also applies to fleets where AI algorithms can analyze data on vehicle usage and maintenance to optimize fleet management, reducing costs and improving efficiency.

Autonomous (Self-Driving) Vehicles

AI-powered autonomous vehicles are a touchy subject these days after recent reports of crashes and accidents, but these cars and trucks can actually be safer and more efficient than traditional forms of transportation by reducing the risk of human error and improving traffic flow. But how are they actually safer?

Human error is a leading cause of car accidents today and autonomous vehicles can eliminate this risk because they are not subject to human fatigue, distraction, or impaired driving.

Through the use of a variety of sensors, cameras, and other technologies to monitor their surroundings, AI-driven vehicles are always aware of potential hazards and can react more quickly and accurately than a human driver.

Autonomous vehicles may also come equipped with additional safety features such as emergency braking, lane departure warnings, and adaptive cruise control, all of which can help prevent accidents and improve overall safety.

My current vehicle features sensors that allow my vehicle to stay between the road lines and remain several car lengths behind the car in front of me when cruise control is on. Do I turn those features on, lift my hands off the wheel, and take a nap? No way! But I have learned to use those features to aid my driving.

It is important to note that autonomous vehicles are still in development, and more testing is needed to fully understand their potential safety benefits and limitations.

Traffic Management

AI can help provide traffic management solutions by analyzing data from various sources to predict and manage traffic flow.

Sensors placed along roads and highways can collect data on traffic volume, speed, and congestion that can be used to identify patterns and make predictions in real time about future traffic flow.

AI can also use this data to optimize traffic flow by adjusting traffic signals in real time, creating better routes for vehicles, and managing traffic in congested areas. An AI system may recommend alternate routes to drivers based on real-time traffic data, helping to reduce congestion on heavily traveled roads.

In addition, AI can help reduce accidents by analyzing data on accident hotspots and making recommendations for improvements such as changes to road design or traffic patterns to reduce the risk of accidents in high-risk areas.

Travel Agency

AI can be used as a travel agency by providing personalized recommendations and booking services to travelers. Travelers can interact with AI chatbots or virtual assistants to receive customized travel recommendations based on their preferences and budget.

AI can use natural language processing and machine learning algorithms to understand traveler preferences and make personalized recommendations for flights, hotels, and activities. An automated travel agent may suggest a list of hotels and activities based on the traveler's preferred location, budget, and travel dates.

AI can also help streamline the booking process by automating and providing instant confirmations. This can save time and reduce the risk of errors or double bookings.

In addition, AI can provide real-time updates to travelers about their trips, such as flight delays or gate changes. This can help travelers stay informed and adjust their plans accordingly.

Shipping, Logistics, and Supply Chain Management

AI can easily be used to optimize shipping routes, reducing travel time and fuel costs. AI algorithms can analyze real-time data on traffic, weather, and other factors to identify the fastest and most efficient routes for shipping goods.

AI can also be used to optimize inventory management by predicting demand for products and ensuring that warehouses and distribution centers have the right inventory on hand. This can help reduce waste and improve customer satisfaction by ensuring that products are available when customers want them.

In addition, AI can help improve supply chain transparency and visibility by providing real-time updates on the status of shipments and deliveries. This can help reduce delays and improve customer satisfaction by providing accurate and up-to-date information on the status of orders.

Environmental Sustainability

AI can help with environmental sustainability in the transportation industry by reducing emissions and improving fuel efficiency. AI algorithms can be used to optimize the routing and scheduling of vehicles, reducing the distance traveled and the amount of fuel consumed.

AI can also be used to optimize the use of alternative fuels and energy sources, such as electric or hybrid vehicles. AI algorithms can analyze data on energy usage and vehicle performance to identify areas for improvement and optimize the use of alternative energy sources.

The proper maintenance of vehicles, especially in a fleet scenario, ensures that they are operating at peak efficiency and reduces the risk of breakdowns or other issues that can lead to increased emissions.

Should Drivers Be Worried About AI-Driven Cars on Public Roads?

Self-driving vehicles are equipped with advanced sensors and algorithms that allow them to perceive their surroundings and make decisions based on real-time data, helping to avoid accidents and reduce human error on the roads.

However, it is important to ensure that self-driving vehicles are safe and reliable before they are deployed on public roads. This requires rigorous testing and validation to ensure that they can operate safely and effectively in a variety of conditions, as well as ongoing monitoring and evaluation to identify and address any issues that may arise.

Drivers and transportation companies should be informed and educated about the use of AI in their industry, including the benefits and potential risks. Drivers should have the opportunity to receive training and support in working with self-driving vehicles, and to express any concerns or feedback about the use of AI in their work.

Chapter Thirteen

AI for the Manufacturing Industry

AI has the potential to transform the manufacturing industry by providing new tools and techniques for efficiency, quality control, and predictive maintenance.

Predictive Maintenance

AI algorithms can analyze data from sensors and other sources to predict when maintenance is needed on machines and equipment, reducing downtime and improving productivity.

Quality Control

AI can be trained to identify defects in products based on images, video, or other data sources. This can help identify defects that may be difficult for humans to detect, such as microcracks or other imperfections.

AI can also be used to improve the consistency of manufacturing processes by analyzing data on production lines and identifying areas for improvement. The AI models can analyze data on the temperature, humidity, and other environmental factors that may affect the quality of products, and make recommendations for adjustments to the manufacturing process to improve product quality.

Monitoring the performance of machines and equipment used in the manufacturing process helps identify potential issues before they lead to defects or other quality issues. This can help reduce downtime and improve the overall efficiency of the manufacturing process.

Autonomous Robots

AI-powered autonomous robots are equipped with sensors, cameras, and other technologies that enable them to navigate and operate autonomously in a manufacturing environment. We already see this technology in major companies like Amazon, which has revolutionized the manufacturing industry in the last 10 years.

AI algorithms can be used to optimize the operation of these robots, enabling them to perform tasks such as assembly, packaging, and quality control with a high degree of accuracy and speed. These robots can work around the clock, without breaks or the need for human supervision (aside from maintenance), increasing the overall productivity of the manufacturing process.

Autonomous robots can also be used to perform tasks that may be dangerous or unpleasant for human workers, such as working in high-temperature environments or handling hazardous materials. This can help improve worker safety and reduce the risk of accidents or injuries.

If these robots find that the layout and flow of the facility could be improved, they can suggest changes for optimization that could boost efficiency and reduce the amount of time and energy required to produce products.

Supply Chain Management

AI can help with supply chain management in the manufacturing industry by optimizing the flow of goods and reducing costs through analyzing data from production, inventory levels, and customer demand to make predictions and recommendations for inventory management and logistics.

AI can enable manufacturers to adjust their production schedules and inventory levels to meet customer needs more effectively by predicting demand for the best- and lowest-selling products. AI can also be used to optimize the routing and scheduling of goods, reducing transportation costs and improving the speed and efficiency of deliveries.

Identifying potential issues before they impact the supply chain is a detrimental part of supply chain management that can be easily handled with AI. This can help manufacturers make adjustments to their sourcing strategies to improve reliability and reduce costs.

Predictive Analytics

AI can help with predictive analytics in the manufacturing industry by analyzing data to make predictions about future outcomes. Predictive analytics can be used to optimize the manufacturing process by identifying potential issues before they occur, reducing downtime, and improving efficiency.

When AI analyzes data on machine performance, it can help identify potential issues before they lead to equipment failures or production delays. This can aid manufacturers in preventative maintenance scheduling and help make adjustments to their production schedules to avoid disruptions.

AI can also be used to predict demand for products, enabling manufacturers to adjust their production schedules and inventory levels to meet customer needs more effectively. This helps reduce waste and improves profitability by ensuring that resources are used efficiently.

The use of resources, such as energy and raw materials, can be guided by AI to reduce waste and improve sustainability. By analyzing data on resource usage and identifying areas for improvement, manufacturers can reduce their environmental impact and improve their bottom line.

Human-Robot Collaboration

Human-robot collaboration in the manufacturing industry involves working together with robots to perform tasks that are difficult or dangerous for humans, while also leveraging human skills and decision-making abilities where they are most needed.

This collaboration can take many forms, from robots assisting human workers with heavy lifting and repetitive tasks, to autonomous robots working alongside human operators in assembly lines or other manufacturing processes. Robots can also be used to perform tasks that require high levels of precision or that involve working with hazardous materials, reducing the risk of injury to human workers.

In a collaborative manufacturing environment, robots can be programmed to work alongside human workers, with the two working together to complete tasks efficiently and effectively. For example, a robot might assist a human worker with a task that requires a high degree of precision, such as assembling small components, while the human worker provides guidance and oversight.

This collaboration can also involve the use of AI algorithms to optimize the workflow and decision-making process, enabling robots and humans to work together more effectively. By leveraging the strengths of both humans and robots, manufacturing companies can improve productivity, reduce costs, and improve worker safety and job satisfaction.

AI and the Labor Force

While some may worry that the use of AI in manufacturing could negatively affect the labor force, it is important to note that AI is not intended to replace human workers but rather to augment their abilities and improve safety. AI-powered robots and machines can be used to perform tasks that are dangerous or difficult for humans, freeing up workers to focus on higher-level tasks that require human judgment and problem-solving skills.

Furthermore, the use of AI in manufacturing can create new job opportunities for workers with the skills and knowledge required to design, develop, and maintain AI-powered systems. Additionally, the increased efficiency and productivity resulting from the use of AI can help to grow the manufacturing industry overall, leading to increased demand for workers across a range of roles.

It is important to ensure that the use of AI in manufacturing is implemented responsibly and ethically, with a focus on minimizing any potential negative impacts on the workforce. This may include providing training and support for workers in adapting to new technologies, ensuring that AI is used in ways that are transparent and accountable, and working with labor unions and other stakeholders to ensure that workers' rights and interests are protected.

AI can help the manufacturing industry to increase efficiency, improve quality control, and optimize supply chain management, ultimately benefiting manufacturers and consumers alike. While there may be concerns about the potential impact on the labor force, it is important to ensure that AI is used responsibly and ethically, with a focus on augmenting human abilities and protecting workers' rights and interests. With careful planning and implementation, AI can help to create a more efficient, productive, and sustainable manufacturing industry.

Chapter Fourteen

AI for Farmers

Farmers have access to tools that their forefathers doing the same job 100 years ago could never imagine. I'm not talking about air-conditioned cabins and GPS navigation in their harvesters, I'm talking about machines helping grow the food we eat.

Crop Monitoring

AI can help farmers with valuable insights into crop health and growth by monitoring crops in real time and identifying potential issues early, enabling them to take corrective action before it's too late.

Sensors and drones can be used to monitor soil moisture levels, temperature, and other environmental factors that affect crop growth. This can help farmers optimize irrigation and fertilization, ensuring that crops receive the right amount of water and nutrients at the right time.

AI can also be used to identify potential issues with crop health, such as pests or diseases. By analyzing images of crops taken by overhead AI-navigated drones or other sensors, the algorithms can identify areas of the field that may be affected by pests or disease, enabling farmers to take action before the problem spreads.

In addition, AI can help farmers predict crop yields based on historical data and environmental factors. By providing farmers with insights into expected yields, AI can help farmers make informed decisions about planting, harvesting, and pricing their crops.

Autonomous Vehicles

I talked a great deal in the Transportation chapter about autonomous vehicles and their benefits, but did you know that self-driving crop harvesters are a thing, too?

Autonomous farm vehicles can be programmed to perform a variety of tasks, such as planting, harvesting, and transporting crops, reducing the need for human workers to perform these tasks manually. This is especially important as concerns over the long-term effects of pesticides and herbicides continue to surface.

Using advanced sensors and GPS technology, AI can ensure that each seed is planted in the right location and at the right depth. This can help improve crop yields and reduce waste.

Autonomous vehicles can also be used to harvest crops, using advanced sensors and algorithms to identify when crops are ready to be harvested and to perform the harvesting process more efficiently than human workers. This can help reduce labor costs and improve productivity.

These vehicles can also be used to transport crops and other materials around the farm, reducing the need for human workers to perform these tasks manually. This can help reduce labor costs and improve efficiency.

Soil Management

AI can help with soil management in the agricultural industry by analyzing data from various sources to provide farmers with valuable insights into soil health and fertility. By analyzing data on soil type, moisture levels, and other environmental factors, AI algorithms can help farmers optimize soil management practices, ensuring that crops receive the nutrients and other inputs they need to grow and thrive.

Soil moisture levels can be monitored to help predict when irrigation is needed. This can help farmers optimize irrigation practices, ensuring that crops receive the right amount of water at the right time.

AI can also be used to analyze soil samples and provide recommendations for fertilizer application. The soil type, nutrient levels, and other data factors help AI to recommend the optimal amount and type of fertilizer to use, improving soil health and crop yields.

AI can help farmers identify areas of the field that may be at risk of erosion or other soil health issues. By analyzing data from sensors and drones, AI algorithms can identify areas of the field that may be at risk and provide recommendations for soil management practices that can help prevent erosion and other issues.

Livestock Management

The health and behavior of animals is a complete science in and of itself, and AI can even help with something as unpredictable and delicate as livestock management. By analyzing sensor data, AI can help farmers monitor the health and well-being of their livestock and identify potential issues before they become more serious.

AI can be used to watch the behavior of cows to identify when they may be in heat or experiencing other health issues. This can help farmers optimize breeding practices, milk production in dairy cattle, and ensure that animals are healthy and productive.

AI can also be used to monitor the feeding and watering of animals, ensuring that they receive the right amount and type of feed and water.

Monitoring the animals' environment, including temperature and humidity levels, is crucial to maintain healthy animals. By analyzing data from sensors, AI algorithms can help farmers ensure that animals are kept in optimal conditions, reducing the risk of disease and other issues.

Food Safety

Farmers and food processors need to be equipped with the right tools to detect and prevent contamination and other food safety issues. AI can provide those tools and help detect potential sources of contamination while identifying areas where food safety risks may be high.

These sources of contamination could originate from food production facilities, pests, or improper sanitation practices. If AI discovers such contamination sources, it can alert staff to take corrective action.

AI can be used to track food products through the entire supply chain, providing farmers and food processors with real-time information about the location and condition of their products. This can help ensure that food products are transported and stored properly, reducing the risk of contamination and other food safety issues.

Weather Forecasting

Weather conditions can greatly affect crop production. AI may not be able to change the weather itself, but it can help forecast upcoming weather by analyzing data from a variety of sources, such as satellite imagery, weather sensors, and historical weather patterns.

This information can be used by AI to predict and adjust for droughts, floods, or extreme temperatures that can affect crop growth and productivity. This can help farmers prepare for and mitigate the impact of adverse weather conditions, reducing the risk of crop failure and financial losses.

AI can also be used to provide farmers with real-time information about local weather conditions, such as temperature, humidity, and precipitation. This can help farmers make more informed decisions about when to plant, harvest, and irrigate their crops, optimizing their growing practices for optimal yield and quality.

AI can help provide personalized recommendations to farmers based on their specific crop types, location, and other factors. This can help farmers tailor their growing practices to local weather conditions, reducing the risk of crop failure and improving overall productivity and profitability.

It is important to note, however, that the adoption of AI in the agriculture industry may require significant investment in technology and infrastructure, as well as training and support for farmers in adapting to new technologies. Additionally, there may be concerns about the potential impact on employment in the agriculture industry, as automation and AI may replace most manual labor.

Should Consumers Fear Food Grown by Robots?

Well, it's not really like that. AI is not directly involved in the raising or growing of food. Rather, AI can be used to optimize various processes in food production, such as crop monitoring, pest management, and irrigation. The safety of food produced using AI-enhanced methods is ultimately determined by the quality of the production process and adherence to food safety regulations, rather than the involvement of AI.

That being said, AI can potentially improve food safety by enabling more efficient monitoring and detection of potential hazards. AI-powered sensors can be used to detect contaminants or pathogens in food production facilities, allowing for early intervention and prevention of outbreaks. Additionally, AI can help to identify areas of risk in the food production process, such as temperature fluctuations or equipment malfunctions, allowing for proactive measures to be taken to prevent contamination.

Ultimately, the safety of food raised by AI-enhanced methods will depend on the same factors that determine the safety of any food product, such as adherence to food safety regulations, quality control measures, and proper handling and storage. While AI has the potential to improve the safety and efficiency of food production, it is not a substitute for responsible food handling and production practices.

Chapter Fifteen

AI for Athletes

A I can be used in many different facets of the sports industry that would focus on everything from improving fan engagement to enhancing the viewing experience and providing valuable insights for coaches and athletes.

Game footage, player stats, and social media interactions all contribute to the data that AI would analyze to improve the entire sports industry. This data can be used to create personalized experiences for fans, such as tailored highlight reels or interactive game simulations.

How AI Can Help Athletes

AI is being increasingly used in the sports industry to help players improve their performance, prevent injuries, and enhance overall gameplay. One way AI can help players is by analyzing large amounts of data to track their movements and provide insights on areas for improvement. AI can identify patterns in a player's movements, such as their running speed and trajectory, and provide feedback on how they can optimize their movements to improve performance.

AI can also be used to predict and prevent injuries by analyzing data on a player's physical condition, such as their heart rate, breathing, and muscle movements. By detecting anomalies in these patterns, AI can alert coaches and trainers to potential injury risks, allowing them to adjust training regimens or rest periods as needed to prevent injuries.

Players can improve their decision-making skills through AI analyzing data on past games and identifying patterns in how certain plays or strategies were successful. By learning from this data, AI can provide real-time advice to players – even during games – to help them make more informed decisions that can increase their chances of success.

How AI Can Help Coaches

AI can be a valuable tool for coaches by providing them with data-driven insights and analysis to improve their team's performance. Evaluating past games, including player and team performance, can be evaluated to identify patterns and trends. This can help coaches make more informed decisions about training regimens, game strategies, and even player selection.

AI can also be used to provide real-time analysis during games, using sensors and cameras to track player movements and provide insights on the opposing team's strengths and weaknesses. By providing this information in real time, coaches can adjust their game strategies and tactics as needed to increase their chances of success.

Furthermore, AI can help coaches with scouting and player recruitment by analyzing data on potential recruits, including their physical abilities and past performance. This can help coaches identify promising talent that may have otherwise gone unnoticed, improving their team's overall performance.

How AI Can Help Fans

AI can provide sports fans with a range of benefits, from personalized recommendations to real-time updates and insights on their favorite teams and players. Certain AI apps can analyze data on past games and player performance to provide personalized recommendations on what games to watch, which teams and players to follow, and even provide real-time updates during games. This can help fans stay up-to-date on the latest developments and make more informed decisions about which games to watch and which players to follow.

Let's use baseball as an example. AI can analyze data on pitch velocity, spin rate, and trajectory to provide real-time insights on a player's performance and provide predictions on how they might perform in future games. This can help fans make informed decisions when placing bets (where it's legal) or predicting the outcomes of games.

Chapter Sixteen

Ethics and Risks of AI

The use of AI for creative projects raises a number of ethical considerations that must be taken into account.

Intellectual Property Rights

When using AI to create new works, there may be questions about who owns the resulting intellectual property, such as the copyright or patent rights.

One of the main issues with AI and intellectual property rights is that it can be difficult to determine who is responsible for the creation of a work. For example, if an AI system creates a new artwork or invention, it may be unclear whether the AI system itself can be considered the creator, or whether the human who developed and trained the AI system should be considered the creator.

In addition, there may be questions about ownership of the data used to train AI systems. If an AI system is trained on data that is protected by intellectual property rights, such as copyrighted material, there may be questions about whether the resulting AI system infringes on those rights.

To address these issues, there have been calls for new regulations and legal frameworks to govern the use of AI and intellectual property. Some experts have suggested that AI-generated works should be treated like collaborative works between humans and machines, with both parties sharing in the ownership and rights to the resulting intellectual property.

The issue of intellectual property rights when using AI is complex and multifaceted, and will likely require ongoing dialogue and collaboration between stakeholders in order to develop fair and effective solutions.

Bias

The issue of bias arises because AI algorithms are often developed based on data sets that may not be representative of the entire population. As a result, AI systems can learn and replicate biases that already exist in society, such as racial or gender bias.

One of the main challenges in addressing bias in AI is identifying and addressing the biases that are present in the data sets used to train AI algorithms. If a data set is biased, the AI system will learn and replicate that bias, potentially leading to unfair or discriminatory outcomes. Another challenge is that bias in AI can be difficult to detect, since AI systems may make decisions based on complex algorithms that are difficult to understand and interpret.

Another challenge is that addressing bias in AI can be costly and time-consuming. It may require additional data collection, pre-processing, or algorithmic adjustments to ensure that the AI system is not biased. Additionally, there is a lack of standardization in the field of AI, which makes it difficult to develop consistent guidelines for addressing bias.

Addressing bias in AI is a complex and ongoing challenge that requires collaboration and interdisciplinary efforts. It requires a thorough understanding of the biases that exist in society, as well as a commitment to developing AI systems that are fair, transparent, and accountable. This will require ongoing dialogue and collaboration between stakeholders in the field of AI, including researchers, policymakers, and industry leaders.

Transparency

Transparency refers to the ability to understand how an AI system arrived at a particular output or decision. This is important because it allows users to assess the reliability and fairness of the AI system and to identify any potential biases or errors that may have been introduced.

One of the main challenges in achieving transparency in AI is the complexity of the algorithms that are used in AI systems. These algorithms can be highly complex and difficult to understand, even for experts in the field. As a result, it can be difficult for users to determine how an AI system arrived at a particular output or decision.

To address this challenge, there is a growing need for greater transparency and explainability in AI systems. This can be achieved through the use of techniques such as machine learning interpretability, which allow users to gain insights into how an AI system arrived at a particular output or decision.

Machine learning interpretability techniques involve analyzing the inputs and outputs of an AI system and mapping them to specific features of the data. This can help users to identify any potential biases or errors that may have been introduced and to understand how the AI system arrived at a particular output or decision.

Achieving transparency in AI is essential for ensuring the reliability and fairness of AI systems. It requires ongoing research and development to develop new techniques for improving the transparency and explainability of AI systems, as well as collaboration between stakeholders in the field of AI to develop guidelines and standards for ensuring transparency in AI.

Human Labor

While there is no doubt that AI has the potential to automate many tasks that are currently performed by humans, there is a great deal of debate about whether AI will take away too many jobs.

One of the main challenges in predicting the impact of AI on human labor is that it is difficult to predict how quickly and to what extent AI will be adopted in various industries and sectors. Some industries, such as manufacturing and transportation, are already highly automated. But other industries, such as healthcare and education, may be less susceptible to job losses due to the fact that they involve more complex and interpersonal tasks.

Another challenge is that AI has the potential to create new jobs and industries that do not currently exist. For example, the development and implementation of AI systems will require a great deal of expertise and knowledge, creating new opportunities for professionals in fields such as computer science, engineering, and data analysis.

While it is difficult to predict the exact impact of AI on human labor, it is unlikely that AI will take away all the jobs. However, it is likely that some jobs will be automated, and it will be important for individuals and society as a whole to prepare for the potential changes and disruptions that may arise as a result. This may involve developing new skills and education programs, creating new social safety nets, and exploring new ways to distribute the benefits of AI technology more equitably.

Unintended Consequences

There may be unintended consequences of using AI in creative projects, particularly if the output is used in a way that harms individuals or communities.

There have been versions of AI tools in place for generations. You might be surprised to learn that many very famous authors use outsourcing and ghostwriting to either create a first draft or somehow aid in the production of their best-selling novels. Is this more or less ethical than using AI in much the same way?

What Are Potential Risks of AI Use Long-Term?

While AI has the potential to bring many benefits to society, there are also potential risks and negative impacts that must be considered. Most of these negative impacts revolve around the possibility of AI self-learning to the point that human intervention becomes obsolete, which is exactly why many are calling for more regulations on AI before things get too out of hand.

Job Displacement

Of course, the big concern is that AI has the potential to automate many jobs, which may lead to job displacement and economic inequality. This could lead to widespread unemployment and a loss of income for many people.

Bias and Discrimination

AI systems are only as unbiased as the data they are trained on. If the data used to train an AI system is biased, the output may also be biased, perpetuating inequalities or harmful stereotypes. This can have negative impacts on individuals and communities, particularly those who are already marginalized.

Privacy and Security

As AI becomes more integrated into our daily lives, there is a risk that personal data may be compromised or used in unethical ways. This can have negative impacts on individuals and society as a whole.

Autonomous Weapons

There is a risk that AI could be used to develop autonomous weapons, which could be used to carry out military operations without human intervention. This could have devastating consequences and could lead to a loss of human life.

Lack of Accountability

As AI becomes more complex, it may become more difficult to understand how it arrives at particular decisions or outputs. This can make it difficult to hold individuals or organizations accountable for the actions of AI systems.

The potential risks and negative impacts of AI in the future require careful consideration and evaluation. It is important for individuals and organizations to approach the development and deployment of AI with caution and sensitivity, and to take steps to mitigate potential risks and negative impacts.

How Can We Be More Ethical with AI Usage?

At this early stage in the AI boom, society is also at a turning point for human ethics. That type of crossroads can be detrimental to the advancement of the technology, both positively and negatively. So what can be done to raise awareness, and what are the biggest ethical concerns?

Diversity and Inclusivity

Ensure that the data used to train AI systems is diverse and inclusive and that the systems themselves are designed to be accessible and beneficial for all users.

Transparency and Explainability

Develop AI systems that are transparent and explainable, so that individuals can understand how decisions are being made and can hold individuals and organizations accountable for the actions of AI systems.

Privacy and Security

Protect personal data and ensure that individuals have control over their own data, including the ability to consent to its use and to request its deletion.

Oversight and Regulation

Establish oversight and regulatory frameworks to ensure that AI is developed and deployed in a responsible and ethical manner.

Human-Centered Design

Develop AI systems that are designed to be human-centered, and that prioritize the needs and well-being of individuals and communities.

Collaboration and Engagement

Engage with stakeholders from diverse backgrounds and perspectives, including individuals who may be impacted by the development and deployment of AI systems.

Continual Monitoring and Improvement

Continually monitor and improve AI systems, to ensure that they remain aligned with ethical principles and do not cause harm.

By following these suggestions, individuals and organizations can ensure that AI is developed and deployed in a responsible and ethical manner, with a focus on benefiting individuals and society as a whole.

CHAPTER SEVENTEEN

WHERE DO WE GO FROM HERE?

AI development is improving and growing every single day. It's growing so quickly that some of what I've written in this book will be obsolete by the time you read it. But this is the main reason I stayed away from getting too specific with product instructions. The important takeaways I wanted to convey are centered around embracing the technology to help improve your business or personal life.

AI technology is never going to be as slow and as primitive as it is right now. We're on the cusp of something really big here, and just the fact that you're reading this book indicates that you believe that, too.

The best thing you can do is grab a free trial of Midjourney or play around with ChatGPT and see what all the hype is really about. Do you feel that what you've heard about AI is true? Do you feel that there are improvements to be made? How could you see yourself utilizing this technology for yourself or your business?

These are all questions that can only be answered by you. You know what's best for you and you know just what aspects of your home or work life could be supplemented by an artificial intelligence assistant.

AI technology is meant to take the human workload to new levels of efficiency and creativity, while properly maintaining arm's length from complete autonomy. As mentioned several times in this book, AI is meant to supplement our workload and not replace it. Sure, it's inevitable that it will replace a few jobs here and there, but this is certainly not a problem exclusive to artificial intelligence.

How we grow and integrate with AI will not only determine our own success but also that of the next generation.

Glossary of Common Terms

Algorithm: A set of instructions or rules that a computer program follows to solve a problem or perform a task.

Artificial Intelligence (AI): The simulation of human intelligence processes by machines, including learning, reasoning, and self-correction.

Artificial Superintelligence (ASI): An advanced form of artificial intelligence that surpasses human intelligence in all areas and activities. It is a hypothetical form of AI that would be capable of performing any intellectual task that a human can, and potentially even surpassing human cognitive abilities in ways that are difficult to imagine. The development of ASI is currently the subject of much debate and speculation, as some experts believe that it could pose an existential risk to humanity if it is not developed and controlled responsibly.

Automation: The use of technology to perform tasks without human intervention.

Big Data: Extremely large data sets that can be analyzed computationally to reveal patterns, trends, and associations.

Bias: The presence of systematic errors or inaccuracies in a machine learning model that can result in unfair or discriminatory outcomes.

Black Box: A term used to describe an AI system where the internal workings are unknown or not easily understood.

Chatbot: A program that uses natural language processing to interact with users in a conversational manner.

Computer Vision: A field of AI that focuses on enabling computers to interpret and understand visual information from the world.

Convolutional Neural Networks (CNNs): A type of neural network commonly used in computer vision tasks such as image recognition.

Deep Learning: A type of ML that uses neural networks with many layers to analyze and extract patterns from large data sets.

Edge Computing: A type of computing where data processing and analysis is done on the device rather than in the cloud.

Ensemble Learning: A technique in machine learning where multiple models are combined to improve the accuracy of predictions.

Ethics of AI: The set of moral principles and values that guide the development and use of artificial intelligence systems.

Explainable AI: The development of AI models and systems that can be easily understood and interpreted by humans.

Fairness: The extent to which an AI system provides equitable outcomes for all individuals or groups.

Generative Adversarial Networks (GANs): A type of deep learning algorithm where two neural networks compete with each other to generate realistic outputs.

Hyperparameters: Parameters set by a programmer that control the learning process of a machine learning algorithm.

Human-in-the-Loop: A system where a human provides input or oversight to an AI system.

Intellectual Property: The legal rights that protect the creations of the mind, such as inventions, literary and artistic works, symbols, names, and images.

Interpretability: The ability to explain how an AI system arrived at a particular decision or prediction.

Machine Learning (ML): A subset of AI that allows computer programs to learn and improve from experience without being explicitly programmed.

Natural Language Generation (NLG): The process of generating human-like language from data or structured information.

Natural Language Processing (NLP): A branch of AI that focuses on the interaction between humans and computers using natural language.

Neural Networks: A set of algorithms that are designed to recognize patterns in data and simulate the behavior of the human brain.

Overfitting: A problem in machine learning where a model is too complex and performs well on training data but poorly on new data.

Privacy: The protection of personal information in AI systems, including the collection, storage, and use of data.

Recurrent Neural Networks (RNNs): A type of neural network commonly used in natural language processing tasks such as language translation.

Reinforcement Learning: A type of machine learning where an agent learns to behave in an environment by performing actions and receiving rewards or punishments.

Robotics: The branch of technology that deals with the design, construction, and operation of robots.

Robustness: The ability of an AI system to perform well in a variety of situations and conditions.

Semi-Supervised Learning: A type of machine learning where the algorithm is trained on both labeled and unlabeled data.

Training Data: Data used to teach a machine learning algorithm how to recognize patterns and make predictions.

Transfer Learning: A technique in machine learning where a model trained on one task is applied to another related task.

Underfitting: A problem in machine learning where a model is too simple and performs poorly on both training and new data.

Unsupervised Learning: A type of machine learning where the algorithm learns patterns and relationships in data without being given specific outputs.

CPSIA information can be obtained
at www.ICGtesting.com
Printed in the USA
BVHW051450230523
664715BV00014B/812